D1636138

over

Warning-Disclaimer

Overturn Turnover

Why some employees leave,

why some employees stay,

and ways to keep the ones

who you want to stay

Paul R. Ahr, PhD, MPA
Thomas B. Ahr, MA, PHR

The Altenahr Group, Ltd.
St. Louis & Miami Beach

ST. LOUIS
CAUSEWAY PUBLISHING
MISSOURI

Causeway Publishing Company
St. Louis, Missouri

Overturn Turnover

Why some employees leave,
why some employees stay,
and ways to keep the ones
who you want to stay

By Paul R. Ahr, PhD., M.P.A.
and Thomas B. Ahr, M.A., PHR

Published by:

Causeway Publishing Company
225 S. Meramec Avenue – Suite 1029
St. Louis, Missouri 63105

Library of Congress Catalog Card Number: 00-092484

Printed by IPC Graphics
Published in the United States of America.

ISBN# 0-9704936-2-2

To our parents who empower us,
our spouses who encourage us,
and our children who inspire us.

Acknowledgements

We would like to sincerely thank the following persons for their assistance in the preparation and publication of this book.

In addition to our spouses who encouraged us, Patricia Forde Ahr and Christine L. Ahr, they are: Kathy A. Carter, Dr. Robert L. Porter, Denis W. Ahr, Dr. Richard B. Zonderman, C. C. LaPrima, Kelly Pingleton, Peg Horrell, Marcel Turner, Marian McCreary, Bob Koch, Dr. Edward J. Cronin, Dorothy Rubick and Dr. Jack Hartstein.

Special thanks go to Peg and George Lestina and their staff at IPC Graphics for turning hundreds of sheets of paper into this real book.

TABLE OF CONTENTS

PREFACE

This is a book about treating employees right. For the past 14 years we have been measuring employee attitudes and advising supervisors and other managers on how to treat their employees in ways that spontaneously increase the job satisfaction and productivity of both – employees and managers.

Several years ago our clients asked us to turn our attention to solving a problem that was soon reaching critical proportions: employee initiated turnover. They wondered whether our experience in employee attitude measurement, forecasting behavior in organizational settings, and preparing supervisors and other managers to improve employee job satisfaction and productivity could help solve this problem.

When we began to address the issue of employee initiated turnover we learned that this was, relatively speaking, a new field of inquiry. The first major writing in this area was published about 40 years ago, and little was done for 15 more years. Happily, there has developed over the past decade a robust body of research on employee commitment (why employees stay) and turnover (why employees leave), which we have attempted to bring together in this book.

Our purpose in writing *Overturn Turnover* is to continue our commitment to advising supervisors and other managers how to treat their employees in ways that spontaneously increase the job satisfaction and productivity of employees, supervisors and managers, alike.

In the thousands of person-to-person exit interviews we have conducted and exit surveys we have read, we have learned that the single best way to retain the employees who you want to keep is to treat them right. Organizations that treat their employees right not only retain their key employees, but also attract desirable job applicants to replace those employees who do leave.

We are grateful to our clients who encouraged us in this work by their professional interest and financial support. There is nothing better in work life than being paid to do what you love to do.

We have been blessed with the opportunity to study the attitudes, opinions and decisions of thousands of employees in scores of organizations over the past 14 years. Each of these persons has helped us better understand why some employees leave the organizations for which they work, why some employees stay, and how better to help supervisors and managers keep the employees who they and their organizations want to stay.

St. Louis, MO
June 5, 2000

PART I: WHY EMPLOYEES LEAVE

Employee initiated turnover of productive workers[1] is a major source of lost productivity and profits in America today. Our work in the area of employee turnover puts us in regular contact with organizations[2] experiencing annual turnover rates of over 20%, with some categories of employees turning over two times per year for a 200% turnover rate! The costs to replace these departed employees can be as much as one third of their annual salaries, or more[3] – if replacements can be recruited at all.

---

[1] The primary focus of this book will be on employee initiated turnover, which is the aggregate effect of the voluntary departure of employees (employee initiated departure) which has not been initiated by the organization and is not seen by the organization as in its best interests. Numerous authors (72, 93, 94, 113, 129) have pointed out the potentially beneficial aspects to organizations of organization initiated employee turnover. The employee initiated turnover discussed in this book tends to be disruptive to organizational functioning and therefore not beneficial to the employing organizations.

[2] Throughout this book we use the term *organization* to refer to an employing group, such as a company, corporation, agency, etc..

[3] Woodruffe (131), citing Whitehead (128) states that the costs to replace some employees exceed $100,000 per resignation.

In this PART we will look at the reasons employees give for leaving their jobs and how these reasons correspond with the real causes of employee initiated turnover in the workplace.

For the past several years we have consulted with and trained human resource (HR) professionals and other managers in many private sector and public sector organizations on how to design and administer studies of the reasons for employee initiated departures[4], and how to interpret the results of these studies.

In the first CHAPTER we will discuss the typical reasons employees give for leaving their jobs, pointing out the extent to which employee initiated turnover is related to circumstances under the influence of employers.

In the second CHAPTER we will review how people decide to leave their jobs in the first place. Do they make snap decisions or is there a predictable process that would allow an employer the opportunity to change an employee's emerging or final decision to leave?

Focusing on the unfolding model of turnover developed by Lee and associates, we will show how a knowledge of workplace shocks and employee scripts and images can help managers reduce employee initiated turnover.

In PART II we will look at the other side of the turnover picture: employees who stay. These two themes will later be joined in PART III to form a comprehensive retention management program.

---

[4] Studies of the reasons for employee initiated departures (here referred to as *exit interviews*) can be conducted through one-on-one interviews using a standardized list of questions (here referred to as *person-to-person interviews*), or through printed questionnaires completed by the departing employee (here referred to as *exit surveys*).

CHAPTER 1 REASONS EMPLOYEES GIVE FOR LEAVING THEIR JOBS

The reasons employees give for leaving their jobs are many and varied. Our review of the exit interview forms developed by various organizations has identified over 60 possible reasons for leaving, many of which are shown in TABLES 1 and 2[5]. When asked why they are leaving, many departing employees list several of these reasons.

The reasons that departing employees give for leaving can vary depending on who asks the question (e.g., the employee's supervisor or an independent interviewer) and when they are asked (e.g., when they decide to leave, at departure, or several months after departing). The perceived confidentiality of their responses also affects the reasons departing employees give when asked why they are leaving their jobs.

TABLE 1 presents, in alphabetical order, a list of common choices provided to departing employees on exit interviews.

---

[5] The 12 reasons for leaving one's job most commonly offered on exit interviews (34) are presented in *italics* in TABLE 1. These reasons will be repeated and serve as the bases for developing retention strategies in CHAPTER 8 (pp. 90-95).

TABLE 1
WHY EMPLOYEES LEAVE

1. *Advancement opportunities*
2. Benefits
3. Commuting time/distance
4. Concerns about the organization's future
5. Fear of job elimination
6. *Geographic location of the job*
7. *Immediate supervisor*
8. Inadequate/insufficient/obsolete equipment
9. Inappropriate/no career path
10. Insufficient/inaccurate performance feedback
11. Involuntary changes in job responsibilities
12. Job challenge
13. Job eliminated
14. *Job itself*
15. Job responsibilities
16. Job security
17. *Job stress*
18. Lack of employee empowerment (autonomy)
19. Lack of resources to satisfactorily complete one's job
20. Limited/lack of development opportunities
21. Little/no sense of accomplishment
22. Not recognized for contributions
23. Organization culture
24. Organization relocation
25. *Organization rules/policies/procedures*
26. *Performance appraisal or performance appraisal methods*
27. Personal career change
28. *Personal relationships with co-workers*
29. Physical or medical reasons
30. Problems associated with work
31. *Personal reasons - other*
32. *Salary/general compensation*
33. Spouse relocation

34. Training I received
35. Upper level management
36. Way I was treated
37. Work content
38. Work environment
39. Work/life balance
40. Working conditions

In some cases, exit interviews mix choices about reasons for leaving with choices about where employees are going. Some of these destinations are presented in TABLE 2.

TABLE 2
WHERE EMPLOYEES GO

1. Better job opportunity[6]
2. Employment in another area
3. Retirement/no longer work
4. Return to school
5. Self employment

PERSPECTIVES ON REASONS FOR LEAVING

The reasons employees leave their jobs can be analyzed according to two primary perspectives:

1. the extent to which an employee has control over his or her decision to leave; and

2. the extent to which the employing organization can influence an employee's decision to stay.

---

[6] The choice "Better job opportunity" is a socially desirable response that yields little information on departing employees' actual work experiences with the organization they are leaving, and should be avoided as a choice in exit interviews.

These conditions are presented visually in FIGURE 1, where an employee's control over the decision to leave is classified as high and low, and his or her employer's influence over that decision is likewise classified as high or low[7].

FIGURE 1
ANALYSIS OF EMPLOYEE/EMPLOYER CONTROL OVER DECISIONS TO LEAVE OR STAY

Employer Organization: Level of Influence Over Employee Decisions to Stay

		High	**Low**
Employee: Level of Control Over Decision To Leave	**High**	**A** Deals primarily with employee initiated (voluntary) departures, where employer actions may prevent/delay turnover.	**C** Deals primarily with employee initiated (voluntary) departures, where employer actions are unlikely to prevent/delay turnover.
	Low	**B[8]** Deals primarily with employer initiated (involuntary) departures.	**D** Deals primarily with employee initiated departures, which tend to be unavoidable by either the employer or the employee.

---

[7] This formulation is similar to that of Abelson (1).

[8] This quadrant represents employees who are asked to leave the organization because of their poor performance, job elimination or prior arrangement (e.g., temporary assignment). Many organizations do not collect exit interview information from these employees. However, such data may identify organizational problem areas, especially when there are high levels of employee dismissals for poor performance in one work unit. The exit interview responses from employees who have been involuntarily terminated from their jobs should be analyzed and reported separately from the responses given by employees who depart voluntarily.

FIGURES 2 and 3 present data generated by responses to a typical exit survey. This data is displayed according to the conditions described in FIGURE 1. In this study, no exit interview data were collected from former employees who were involuntarily terminated (quadrant B).

Respondents were asked to identify in priority order their reasons for leaving. FIGURE 2 classifies departed employees' *primary* reasons for leaving. FIGURE 3 classifies *all* the reasons they gave for leaving.

It is interesting to note that more than half (54%) of the primary reasons for leaving (FIGURE 2) and nearly three fourths (73.5%) of the overall reasons for leaving (FIGURE 3) fall in quadrant A. These data suggest that this employer may have been in a position to influence a majority of these employees to stay in their jobs, but did not do so. In our experience, these results are not an uncommon distribution of departing employees' responses.

In EXERCISE 1, list findings from the exit study presented in FIGURES 2 and 3 that you consider important, as well as steps this organization might take to reduce unwanted turnover.

FIGURE 2
PRIMARY REASON FOR LEAVING: AN EXAMPLE

Employer: Level of Influence Over Employee Decisions to Stay

	High	**Low**
High	10%: Management 10%: How you were treated 9%: Salary 8%: Supervisor 4%: Work/personal life balance 3%: Job challenge 3%: Advancement opportunity 3%: Workload 1%: Career development 1%: Recognition for contributions 1%: Work content 1%: Working conditions 0%: Benefits 0%: Policies & procedures **Total = 54%**	17%: Retirement 3%: Commuting distance 0%: Return to school 0%: Start own business **Total = 20%**
Low		10%: Family circumstances 9%: Illness/physical condition **Total = 19%**

Employee: Level of Control Over Decision to Leave

FIGURE 3
ALL REASONS FOR LEAVING: AN EXAMPLE

**Employer: Level of Influence Over Employee
Decisions to Stay**

	High	Low
Employee: Level of Control Over Decision to Leave — High	13%: How you were treated 12%: Management 8%: Salary 7%: Supervisor 7%: Advancement opportunity 5%: Workload 4%: Work/personal life balance 4%: Recognition for contributions 4%: Policies & procedures 3%: Career development 2%: Job challenge 2%: Work content 2%: Working conditions .5%: Benefits **Total = 73.5%**	11%: Retirement 2%: Commuting distance 1%: Start own business .5%: Return to school **Total = 14.5%**
Low		6%: Illness/physical condition 4%: Family circumstances **Total =10%**

EXERCISE 1
OBSERVATIONS ON EXIT INTERVIEW DATA

In the left column below (Findings)*, list findings from the exit study presented in* FIGURES *2 and 3 that you consider important. In the right column* (Remedies)*, list steps this organization might take to reduce unwanted turnover.*

Findings	Remedies
•	•
•	•
•	•
•	•
•	•
•	•
•	•
•	•
•	•
•	•
•	•
•	•
•	•
•	•
•	•

LIMITATIONS TO EMPLOYEES' EXIT INTERVIEW RESPONSES

Employee candor is the goal of exit interviewing. Factors that may impact on employee candor include:

Limitation #1: The most convenient and inexpensive way
Convenience to collect exit interview data may be by
vs. having the departing employee's supervisor
Expense conduct the interview.

Because exit interview responses are influenced by the relationship the employee has with the interviewer, the more removed the interviewer is from direct supervision of the interviewee, the more exit interview responses tend to be candid (41).

The use of other organizational personnel or outside (3rd party) exit interview specialists usually generate more candid responses from departing employees. In many cases, the cost for 3rd party interviewers is less than full time staff assigned to administer an exit interview program.

Limitation #2: The offer of confidentiality impacts on the
Confidentiality candor and number of responses. The less
vs. likely that there will be retaliation or any
Immediate other adverse reaction to a candid response,
Utility the more exit interview responses tend to be
candid.

However, confidential interviews sometimes uncover activities of remaining employees that are illegal, unethical or otherwise may put the organization at risk of legal action or further resignations. Immediate personnel actions taken against the persons identified as rule breakers in an exit interview may be linked to the departing employee, jeopardizing the candor of responses from employees who subsequently depart.

In some organizations, the confidentiality of exit interview responses does not extend to departing employee's allegations of illegal or unethical acts by co-workers. Despite being cautioned about such a limitation to the confidentiality of their responses (see opposite page), some departing employees, nevertheless, volunteer information about perceived illegal or unethical acts committed by others in the organization

Organization management should have in place a plan for dealing with immediate problems that have been identified through exit interviews. This plan should address how serious problems can be resolved as soon as possible without compromising the confidentiality of departing employees' responses.

Limitation #3: Recentness vs. Reflection Ideally, supervisors would be aware of an employee's interest in quitting early enough to influence their subordinate's decision to leave. Generally, information on the job satisfaction of *current* employees only is available in aggregate form from focus groups and employee attitude studies. Therefore, these types of employee feedback may not be detailed enough to help a supervisor who is trying to identify specific employees who are thinking of leaving their jobs.

The reasons employees give for leaving may change as they get ready to depart. For example, an employee who decides to get a new job because he feels that he is poorly treated, and who eventually leaves for a better paying position, may state at departure that he is leaving for better pay.

After leaving, the reasons former employees give for departing may also change (39, 60). Employees' retrospective understanding of why they left and/or explanations for leaving may change as they become familiar with the advantages and disadvantages of their new employment (or retirement) experiences.

Sample Introductory Comments Regarding the Limits of Confidentiality

We believe that open, two-way communication is important to the continued success of [the organization]. This exit interview is an opportunity for you to provide information and voice your opinions and feelings about your job, your department and [the organization] as a whole.

We are interested in knowing the reasons you have for leaving [the organization] so that we can identify the root cause(s) for your departure, and [the organization] can take appropriate actions and develop effective retention strategies. Your comments will remain confidential. Information reported to [the organization] will be limited to numerical and trend data that will not identify either you or your responses.

Please note that there is one exception to this provision of confidentiality. Should you provide us with information that suggests potentially illegal or unethical behavior(s), then we must immediately report your name and that information to [the organization], because [the organization] must investigate any such allegation(s).

We appreciate your time and your candid participation in this exit interview process. Please accept our best wishes for success in your future endeavors.

For many organizations, the most practical way to collect information on the reasons why their employees leave is through an exit interview conducted at or near the date of departure. Research on hindsight bias summarized by Weick (127) provides important support for conducting exit interviews as near to the point in time when the employee leaves as possible. This research documents that persons who are already aware of the outcome of a complex history of events tend to distort the relative importance of prior events to conform them to the ultimate outcome.

Managers have available to them many choices concerning the timing of exit studies and the ways in which this important information can be collected and reported. These choices are discussed in detail in Chapter 7.

SUMMARY

Knowing the reasons why their employees voluntarily leave their jobs is an important element in supervisors' and other managers' efforts to manage turnover in their organizations. Properly designed and administered exit interviews can provide a wealth of information on employees' reasons for leaving.

Special analyses of exit interview data can help direct employers to develop retention interventions that have a higher likelihood of success. One useful approach sorts employee reasons for leaving based on the extent to which (a) employees control their decisions to leave and (b) their employers can influence those decisions.

Considerations such as who conducts the exit interview, when it is conducted, and how confidential information is handled can impact on the candor and reliability of departing employees' responses.

CHAPTER
2
HOW EMPLOYEES DECIDE TO LEAVE THEIR JOBS

The processes by which employees decide to leave their current jobs are multiple and complex. Traditional theories of how employees make these decisions derive from the work of March & Simon (66), and focus primarily on two variables:

1. perceived ease of movement or job availability ("How easy is it for me to find another job?"); and

2. perceived desirability of movement or job dissatisfaction ("How dissatisfied am I with my current job?").

According to the proponents of these theories, employee resignations increase as job availability and job dissatisfaction increase.

THE REAL IMPORTANCE OF JOB AVAILABILITY AND JOB DISSATISFACTION

A critical issue in understanding the reasons for employee initiated turnover is the extent to which job dissatisfaction and job availability separately and together explain departure behavior. The impact of job availability on employee initiated turnover is quite important since the availability of job alternatives *is outside the control of the employing organization.* If job availability is the critical determinant of employee initiated turnover, organizations operating in situations of high job availability may need especially to step up efforts to lower employee dissatisfaction if they intend to control turnover.

This situation suggests that for employees classified in quadrant D of FIGURE 4, lowering job dissatisfaction will not assure increased retention if job availability is a more powerful influence on turnover than job dissatisfaction. Nevertheless, employers *should* try to accommodate all reasonable employee requests for improvements to their work situations, regardless of the quadrant in which the employees might be classified.

FIGURE 4
LIKELIHOOD OF EMPLOYEE INITIATED TURNOVER

Job Availability		Job Dissatisfaction	
		Low	High
	Low	**A** Lowest probability of turnover. Fewest accommodations required of employers.	**C** Medium probability of turnover. Appropriate responses by the employer will reduce turnover in some cases[9].
	High	**B** Medium probability of turnover. Few opportunities for accommodation by employers.	**D** Highest probability of turnover. Employers must address job dissatisfaction.

[9] Employers should try to accommodate reasonable employee requests for adjustments to their work situations. See especially Hulin, et al. (44) and Mobley (82).

INTERVENING THEORIES

In the years since March & Simon's seminal writings, social scientists have focused on the ways in which job availability and job dissatisfaction interact to result in turnover behavior. Such research has demonstrated that the decision to leave one's job involves more variables than simply these two.

For example, some authors (116) have demonstrated that, under certain circumstances, the availability of attractive alternatives can stimulate employee dissatisfaction with their current jobs by creating expectations that are not currently being met by their present jobs.

Other authors (45, 97, 102, 103, 114) have identified the intention to quit as an important component in the ultimate decision to stay or leave.

Finally, some contemporary studies on turnover (44, 56, 57, 58, 59, 60, 61, 102) document employees who leave their jobs without a replacement job lined up. These findings suggest that job dissatisfaction is more important than job availability in determining whether an employee leaves his or her current job.

THE UNFOLDING MODEL OF EMPLOYEE INITIATED TURNOVER

The complex process by which employees decide to leave their jobs has been detailed by Lee and associates (56, 57, 58, 59, 60, 61). According to their unfolding model of turnover, job dissatisfaction, and to a lesser extent job availability, continue to play crucial roles in the decision to leave.

The unfolding model of employee initiated turnover introduces several important concepts, including the following:

1. **Shocks.** According to Lee, et al. (60), shocks to the system (shocks) are specific events that disrupt the regularity of the employee's work situation and that initiate the psychological processes by which an employee decides whether to quit or stay in his or her current job. Shocks may be personal or organizational, pleasant or unpleasant, expected or unexpected. Examples of shocks are presented in EXERCISE 2, which includes places to add examples of other shocks.

EXERCISE 2
SHOCKS

Examples of shocks are:

- Becoming pregnant

- Getting admitted to college

- Getting a new boss

- Getting passed over for promotion

- Buying a larger house

- Resignation of a best friend at work

- Being relocated to another city because of your job

Other examples of shocks are:

-

-

-

-

-

2. **Scripts.** Scripts are plans of action, or scenarios, that individuals develop in advance of an event or situation that they imagine may occur involving them. Scripts are based on the person's prior experience, observation of others, advice from others, reading or social expectations. Scripts detail for a person how he or she should act if confronted with a specific set of circumstances. Examples of scripts are presented in EXERCISE 3, which also includes places to add other scripts.

EXERCISE 3
SCRIPTS

Examples of scripts are:

- If I become pregnant, I'll get a job that has a day care center.

- If I get admitted to school, I will work only part-time.

- If Joe becomes my boss, I'll retire.

- If I don't get promoted in the next 18 months, I'll look for another job.

- If I don't get a salary increase in the next 3 months, I'll look for another job.

Other scripts may include:

-
-
-
-
-

3. **Image Violations.** Image theory (16) proposes that, when confronted with options, people engage first in a somewhat rapid screening of available options. This screening is based on a comparison of the available options against three internal images.

- **Value images** consist of internalized standards of conduct and expectations, that (a) define acceptable and unacceptable beliefs and behaviors, and (b) significantly impact on one's actions and intended actions.

- **Trajectory images** represent an individual's personal vision or agenda for the future in the form of personal goals. Personal goals are important because they organize, direct and propel personal behavior.

- **Strategic images** entail the steps the person believes will prove to be the best route to accomplishing his or her personal goals.

According to image theory, when presented with a new situation or option, a person compares it to his or her value, trajectory and/or strategic images. If the situation or option corresponds to one of these three images it remains viable for comparison with the status quo. Situations or other options that sufficiently conflict with these images are rejected as not viable for comparison with the status quo and are avoided or discarded.

EXERCISE 4 provides an opportunity to consider the relationship between shocks and their impact on value, trajectory and strategic images in work related settings.

EXERCISE 4
SHOCKS AND VALUE, TRAJECTORY AND STRATEGIC IMAGES

*Think about your own career, and/or the careers of persons you know.
What have been/could be shocks in those cases? What personal value,
trajectory and/or strategic images might be challenged by these shocks?*

Shocks	Value, trajectory and/or strategic images challenged

FOUR PATTERNS OF DECIDING TO LEAVE ONE'S JOB

The unfolding model identifies four patterns of deciding whether to leave one's job (60).

1. When confronted with a shock (either work or personally related, either good or bad), some employees apply a known script to the situation. Depending on the match between the shock and the script these employees decide whether to stay or leave. If an employee decides to leave he or she does so based on a personal script and not on the basis of his or her attachment to the organization or after considering alternatives. This pattern is called Path #1.

2. Other employees, when confronted with a shock to their current work situations, reassess their basic attachments to their organizations in terms of their value, trajectory and/or strategic images. Based on these reassessments, if the employees believe that their images no longer fit with their organizations, they leave. These departure decisions do not to tend take alternatives into consideration. This pattern is called Path #2.

3. When confronted with a shock, still other employees consider whether they are capable of forming an attachment with another organization. They evaluate the fit between their current situations and their value, trajectory and/or strategic images.

   If an employee's value, trajectory and/or strategic images no longer fit with those of his or her organization, he or she considers other options. The employee compares these options (which may include not working at all) with his or her current situation until he or she uncovers a better situation that is available. At that time the employee leaves. This pattern is called Path #3.

4. Over time some employees simply get generally dissatisfied with their jobs or working conditions and leave. Some of these employees leave after considering alternatives (Type 4B), and others leave without making any further plans for employment (Type 4A). This pattern, called Path #4, most closely resembles the course of traditional theories of employee initiated turnover. According to Lee and colleagues (60), as many as one-fourth of departing employees can follow Path #4.

IMPLICATIONS FOR REDUCING TURNOVER OF THE UNFOLDING MODEL

A clear understanding of the processes by which employees decide to leave their jobs allows their supervisors and other managers to develop and implement approaches to retain these employees.

The four paths of the unfolding model and the implications for reducing turnover of each path are shown in FIGURE 5. Opportunities for supervisors and other managers to better understand how their employees typically deal with shocks are presented in parentheses in the right column (Implications for Reducing Turnover).

These insights are especially valuable for employees who tend to follow Path #3, since these employees typically consider a range of options, including staying, when confronted with shocks and image violations. Efforts to improve working conditions for these employees, who can account for nearly two-thirds of departing employees (60), may result in a substantial portion of them deciding to remain with the organization (44, 82).

24

FIGURE 5
THE UNFOLDING MODEL OF
EMPLOYEE INITIATED TURNOVER

Path	Decision Path Characteristics	Implications for Reducing Turnover

#1: Shock→Recall→Script→Action (Match=Enact Script)

- A shock to the system elicits a recollection of a similar shock, situation or response (actual or vicarious).

- The shock prompts thoughts about the circumstances, likely actions and their consequences (a script).

- If a script is available, a match occurs, and the script is enacted. If there is no script (or match), another decision path may be initiated.

- Catalogue the shocks departing employees state they have experienced (e.g., through exit interviews or focus groups).

- Minimize the shocks.

- Determine common scripts among employees (e.g., through exit interviews or focus groups).

#2: Shock→Review Basic Attachment→Evaluation→ Action (Misfit=Departure)

- A shock prompts an employee to reassess the quality of his or her basic attachment to the organization.

- Catalogue the shocks departing employees state they have experienced.

- The employee may have scripts that are not acted upon.

- The shock and accompanying situation are judged against three images of compatibility or fit:
  1. value image(s);
  2. trajectory image(s);
  3. strategic image(s).

- If the shock and its information cause the employee to believe that there is a misfit between his or her images and the current job situation, he or she quits. If there is no serious discrepancy, he or she stays.

- Minimize the shocks.

- Supervisors should be aware of the value, trajectory and strategic images of their employees (e.g., through recruitment interviews, supervision or career planning/development).

#3: Shock→Consider Another Attachment→ Evaluation→Search→Analysis→Action

- A shock signals an employee to assess whether a basic attachment could form with another organization.

- The evaluation (as in #2) involves the shock, situation and images. A determination of no fit signals to the employee some dissatisfaction.

- Catalogue departing employees' shocks.

- Minimize the shocks.

- Supervisors should be aware of the value, trajectory and strategic images of their employees (e.g., through career planning/development).

- The dissatisfaction prompts the search for job alternatives. These alternatives are evaluated for fit (or lack of fit) with the images. No-fit eliminates that option. Fit prompts further scrutiny.

- The surviving alternatives (including staying) are subjected to an analysis based on the subjective probability of gaining another more satisfying job or non-work alternative.

- Discuss with employees who express an interest in other jobs ways to make their current job more attractive (e.g., through career planning/development).

#4:   Erosion of Satisfaction/Commitment→Departure

- No shock.

- Erosion of satisfaction and/or commitment over time.

- Some employees simply quit (Type 4-A). Others use more systematic approaches to decide whether to stay, and which options to take on departure (Type 4-B).

- Measure and match employee attitude findings to exit interview results (e.g., through employee attitude studies and exit interviews).

SUMMARY

Early theories explaining how employees decide to quit their jobs focused on two variables: job availability and job dissatisfaction. Research over the intervening 40 years has demonstrated that the decision to leave involves more than these two variables.

The unfolding model details four paths by which employees decide to leave their jobs. In addition to the traditional approach which considers general job dissatisfaction as an important determinant of the decision to leave, the unfolding model also shows how shocks to the system interact with employees' pre-existing scripts or images to create three other decision making styles.

By being aware of (a) their employees' levels of dissatisfaction, (b) the events that would serve as shocks for their employees, and (c) their employees' scripts and images, supervisors and other managers can better anticipate employees' desire to leave and take steps to prevent unwanted turnover.

PART II: WHY EMPLOYEES STAY

Even if as many as one fourth of an organization's employees depart in a given year, three fourths would still remain. Why do some employees go while others stay? Who are the people who stay and why do they do so?

In the next three CHAPTERS we will focus on the issue of employee commitment to the organization. In CHAPTER 3, Meyer and Allen's concepts of the three bases of commitment will serve as a frame for displaying research on the behaviors of committed employees, and the conditions that are associated with varying forms of commitment.

Applying research findings on why employees leave *and* stay, we address the question of how to create a retention oriented work environment utilizing two of our models for employee job satisfaction and productivity. They are the **MORALE**™ model for all employees (CHAPTER 4), and the **SOS** model for successfully incorporating new employees into the productive work of the organization (CHAPTER 5).

In the final PART we will match these research based findings with other management approaches to recommend strategies for managing employee initiated turnover in the organization.

CHAPTER 3 PROMOTING COMMITMENT TO THE ORGANIZATION

The answer to the question of why people stay in organizations is typically found in the research on employees' commitment to their employing organizations. Understanding employee commitment is a complex topic for several reasons.

First, there are multiple definitions of commitment in an organizational setting. However, these multiple definitions do tend to share a common perspective of commitment (73) as a psychological state that:

1. describes the basis of an employee's relationship with the organization; and

2. influences the employee's decision to stay with or leave the organization.

Second, as Lawler (55) points out, organizations are not monolithic entities. Rather, they are composed of multiple subgroups, or what Reichers (99) refers to as various "coalitions and constituencies." Each of these coalitions or constituencies may have, and promote commitment to, its own goals and values. These sub-group goals and values may not be compatible with the goals and values of the organization itself.

Nevertheless, the focus of this book is on employee commitment to the organization itself, its leadership and the ways in which these leaders attempt to carry out the organization's mission. This is the typical focus of measuring commitment to the organization as a whole (74).

A third challenge lies in identifying the different bases for commitment held by different employees. Meyer & Allen (74) identify three components or bases of commitment. Each of these components may be present to some extent in each member of the organization.

Affective Commitment   This component of employee commitment is the one most desired by employers: commitment based on a firm connection between the employee and the organization. Individuals who display high levels of affective commitment strongly identify with the organization and are highly involved with its activities. Employees who have strong levels of affective commitment **want to** belong to or remain with their organizations.

Normative Commitment   This component of commitment is based on an employee's feeling of personal obligation to continue his or her employment with the organization. Employees who demonstrate strong levels of normative commitment feel that they **ought to** belong to or remain with their organizations.

Continuance Commitment   Some employees remain with their employing organizations because they believe that they cannot do better with another employer.

Continuance commitment is based on employees' awareness of the costs to them associated with leaving their organizations. Employees who exhibit strong levels of continuance commitment feel that they **need to** belong to or remain with their organizations.

In EXERCISE 5 consider persons you know who demonstrate affective, normative and continuance commitment to the organizations where they work. What characteristics do they display that leads you to that opinion?

EXERCISE 5
BASES OF COMMITMENT TO THE ORGANIZATION

In the rows below, list the characteristics of persons who you know who display affective, normative and/or continuance commitment in their jobs.

Think about	His/her/their characteristics
Employee(s) with affective commitment	
Employee(s) with normative commitment	
Employee(s) with continuance commitment	

Studies of these components of commitment have identified a wide range of employee behaviors that are correlated significantly with affective commitment to the organization. Fewer behaviors have been found to be correlated with normative and continuance commitment. Some of these correlations are presented in TABLE 3. The studies cited in TABLE 3 document employee behaviors that are either positively or negatively correlated with the various components of commitment.

As with all correlation studies, these findings presume neither that commitment causes the behavior, nor that the behavior causes commitment. Rather, they document behaviors that co-occur either directly (positive correlation shown in TABLE 3 as "+") or inversely (negative correlation shown in TABLE 3 as "—") with high or low levels of affective, normative and continuance commitment.

A review of the behaviors detailed in TABLE 3 reinforces the desirability of attracting and retaining employees who have high levels of affective commitment to the organization. Employees who demonstrate high levels of continuance commitment have been documented to display behaviors that are generally less attractive to employers.

TABLE 4 displays employee characteristics (items #1-#6, #21 & #22) and organizational conditions (items #7-#20) that are antecedents of affective commitment[10]. TABLE 5 displays employee antecedents of continuance commitment. The data presented in Tables 4 and 5 suggest that strategies to reduce unwanted turnover and extend the tenure of productive employees should seek to recruit persons with the following characteristics. They should be persons with (a) a strong work

---

[10] According to Allen & Meyer (6), the work experiences that predict affective commitment tend to predict, to a lesser extent, normative commitment.

TABLE 3

CORRELATIONS OF TYPES OF COMMITMENT WITH
ORGANIZATIONAL BEHAVIORS OF EMPLOYEES

Type[11]	r[12]	Organizational Behavior
A	+	Altruistic acts toward others in the organization/ organizational citizenship (36, 73, 75, 83, 91, 92)
A	+	Avoidance of "budgetary slack" in financial planning (89)
A	+	Compliance with strategic decisions made at the corporate level (52)
A	+	Cost control (24)
A	+	Customer service (86)
A	+	Job performance (15, 22, 49, 75, 77, 83, 104, 105)
A	+	Rating of suitability for promotion (77)
A	+	Sales performance (13)
A	+	Supervisor's ratings of employee dependability and initiative (7)
A	+	Work effort (19, 46, 63, 98, 104)
A	—	Absence frequency [but not number of days] (33)
A	—	Voluntary absence (40, 75, 112)
N	+	Organizational citizenship (73)
N	+	Self report of work effort (10, 98)
N	—	Voluntary absence (75)
C	+	More likely to stay (6)
C	—	Altruism and compliance behavior at work (91)
C	—	Commendations for work (40)
C	—	Organizational citizenship (109)
A&C	—	Absence days annexed to weekends/holidays (112)

[11] A = Affective Commitment, C = Continuance Commitment, N = Normative Commitment

[12] r = correlations, where: "+" represents a positive correlation (High attribute ↔ high commitment; low attribute ↔ low commitment) and "—" represents a negative correlation (High attribute ↔ low commitment; low attribute ↔ high commitment).

TABLE 4
ANTECEDENTS TO AFFECTIVE COMMITMENT

Positive correlations

1. Organizational tenure (69)
2. Age[13] (69)
3. High need for achievement (18)
4. Strong work ethic (18)
5. Perception of one's own competence (69)
6. Predisposition to commitment (57, 87)
- -
7. Decentralization (14, 84)
8. Perception of the fairness of policies/treatment (31, 116) (pay: 106; drug testing: 53; strategic decision making: 53)
9. Adequacy of explanations for company policies (54)
10. New employees who think the organization supports them (5)
11. Leader expresses consideration for employees (24, 69)
12. Supervisor supportiveness (85, 130)
13. Leader-member act as if interdependent [leader-member exchange] (66)
14. Employees who believe their jobs are secure (9)
15. Congruence of employee and organizational goals (99, 121, 123)
16. Participation in decision making (26, 101)
17. Latitude or discretion over activities (24, 37)
18. Task autonomy (26)
19. Receptiveness of management to employee ideas (4)
20. Job scope (65, 69, 76)

Negative correlations

21. Perceived role conflict (22, 24, 69)
22. Perceived role ambiguity (22, 24, 69)

---

[13] This may reflect differences in predisposition to commitment based on age (e.g., if older persons have a higher predisposition to commitment).

TABLE 5
ANTECEDENTS TO CONTINUANCE COMMITMENT

Negative correlations

1. Employees' perceptions of the transferability of their skills (4, 130)
2. Employees' perceptions of employment opportunities available to them (4, 76)

---

ethic and (b) a high need for achievement who, (c) are aware of their own competence and (d) have a predisposition to making and keeping commitments.

Such employees will be more likely to form and sustain a productive commitment to an organization that they perceive acts fairly towards all, provides adequate explanations for company actions, and has leaders and managers who support them. These employees will also form and sustain a productive commitment if they feel that their jobs are secure and that they have an opportunity to participate in the design and implementation of their work activities.

Employees who may be predisposed to forming affective attachments to their workplace will be less inclined to do so if they are unsure of what is expected of them (role ambiguity) or are expected to perform tasks that are incompatible with each other (role conflict).

Finally, employees who demonstrate continuance commitment tend to believe that their skills are not transferable to other jobs, and that few employment opportunities are available to them.

SUMMARY

Research studies on commitment to the organization provide important insights into the reasons why employees continue their employment with their current organizations. Some stay out of loyalty (normative commitment) and others because the costs to them of leaving are more than they are willing to pay (continuance commitment). Those employees who display work attitudes and habits most desired by managers tend to be the ones who remain because they want to (affective commitment).

CHAPTER 4   BUILDING A RETENTION ORIENTED ENVIRONMENT

A retention oriented environment is one that focuses on the work related satisfaction and commitment of productive employees. In this section we have sorted the research findings on employee job satisfaction and commitment into six primary categories. These areas are represented by the acronym **MORALE™** (2).

MORALE™ describes ways that organizations can improve the job satisfaction, productivity and commitment of their employees.	**M**ONEY **O**PPORTUNITIES **R**ELATIONSHIPS **A**DAPTABILITY **L**EADERSHIP **E**QUITY	*The six strategies of the MORALE™ model can be applied to the design of a work-place oriented to retaining key and other employees.*

The relationships among the six **MORALE**™ characteristics are represented in FIGURE 6. In this FIGURE, the **MORALE**™ characteristics are presented in an arrangement that places MONEY at the bottom of the display and EQUITY at the top, with RELATIONSHIPS covering the major portion of one side. This display was chosen to visually represent these three aspects of the **MORALE**™ model:

MONEY: Like the category of physiological needs in Maslow's (68) pyramidal hierarchy of human needs, MONEY is a basic condition of employee satisfaction which, if not satisfactorily met, will eventually lead to employee withdrawal, either through resignation or reduced productivity (44).

RELATIONSHIPS: This category is presented in this way to underscore the critical importance of RELATIONSHIPS in job satisfaction, productivity and commitment to the organization.

EQUITY: The EQUITY category is presented at the top of this chart to represent both (a) the overall importance of perception of fairness at work to employees' decisions to stay at or leave their jobs, and (b) the recognition that employees base their assessment of EQUITY at work on the ways in which MONEY, OPPORTUNITIES, RELATIONSHIPS, ADAPTABILITY AND LEADERSHIP are handled there.

FIGURE 6
MORALE™ : A MODEL FOR EMPLOYEE JOB
SATISFACTION, PRODUCTIVITY AND COMMITMENT

EQUITY	
LEADERSHIP	**RELATIONSHIPS**
ADAPTABILITY	
OPPORTUNITIES	
MONEY	

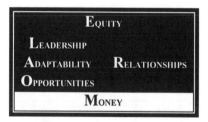

MONEY refers to all forms of employee compensation, including salary, bonuses, benefits and perquisites.

MONEY is a basic requirement for employee satisfaction and productivity. If an employee's need for **MONEY** is not met by his or her employer, the employee will often seek other ways to supplement it.

- Some former employees cite inadequate benefits and/or salaries (i.e., **MONEY**) as the prime reason for their resignations (25, 43, 110).

- An employee's need for **MONEY** may be different at different times in his or her lifetime.

- **MONEY** can satisfy higher order needs (68) such as achievement or self-actualization (17).

- **MONEY** is a prime basis for personal happiness (17).

- The perception that others performing similar work for more **MONEY** is demoralizing (78, 79, 107, 116).

- Prior salaries influence the perceived adequacy of current pay (44, 111), especially if they were great enough to establish a higher standard of living or inflated sense of self worth (54, 78).

- Special monetary incentives including bonuses, cash awards, stock or special budgets for equipment, training or travel discourage the departures of key personnel (42).

- Pension coverage and accumulation deter employees from quitting (47, 81).

The viability of voluntary organizations attest to the power of factors other than **MONEY** to generate commitment and good performance. These factors are detailed in the remaining **MORALE**™ components.

OPPORTUNITIES refer to the chances and choices an organization offers its employees to improve their performance, satisfaction and commitment.

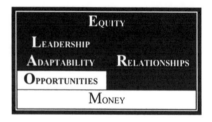

The prospect of opportunities for *advancement* (e.g., job promotion) or *enhancement* (e.g., additional compensation, job enrichment, training, education or other development activities) promote commitment to the organization by extending the horizon of future interactions (11). Employees who are the beneficiaries of advancement or enhancement opportunities are less inclined to leave than are employees who do not receive such benefits.

- Commitment to the organization is positively related to employees' perceptions of employment **OPPORTUNITIES** available to them (4, 76).

- The anticipation that one's current job will lead to better job **OPPORTUNITIES** is a dis-incentive to leave (82).

- The lack of **OPPORTUNITIES** elsewhere discourages employees from leaving (82). However, better **OPPORTUNITIES** outside the organization will promote resignations.

- Actual promotions are positively related to retention (32, 115).

- The lack of promotions weakens commitment (69) and is a prominent contributor to employees' decisions to quit (19).

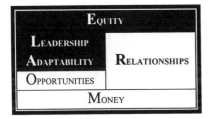

RELATIONSHIPS at work refer to ways of interacting with co-workers, supervisors and other managers.

RELATIONSHIPS are important to organizational functioning because most work is accomplished through the cooperative efforts of a group, on a regular basis, over a long period of time.

- Good **RELATIONSHIPS** with co-workers, as evidenced by having friends at work and having satisfying interactions with co-workers, decrease turnover (20, 96, 97).

- The degree to which newcomers receive positive (investiture) or negative (divestiture) support from experienced co-workers is associated with commitment to the organization (5, 10, 50).

- Employee perceptions of job socialization experiences are positively related to commitment to the organization (5, 10, 12, 50, 80).

- Employee perceptions of support from co-workers are strongly linked to affective commitment (27, 39, 108, 109).

- Perceived supportiveness among co-workers decreases perceived role stress (119).

- Excessive premature employee quitting indicates incomplete organizational socialization (29, 30, 42).

- Co-workers' resignations may undermine the social integration at work and stimulate more turnover (95).

In an environment where change is the only constant, employees and organizations must be flexible, **ADAPTABLE,** and able to tolerate differences.

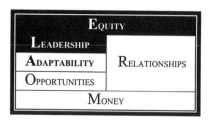

Because the abilities to (a) tolerate ambiguity and uncertainty, (b) embrace differences, and (c) successfully manage reactions to change do not reside in organizations, but rather in the people who comprise them, it is in the best interests of an organization to foster these adaptive abilities in its employees.

- Job stress predicts turnover (42).

- The ability of employees to manage the conflicts of their various roles (e.g., parent, spouse, worker) is important to being able to perform successfully on their jobs (42).

- Realistic job previews reduce turnover when they (a) display the positive and negative aspects of a job and (b) allow a candidate to **ADAPT** to the job (71, 93, 100, 125).

- Job enrichment approaches that focus on skills, task identity and autonomy (42) are more effective in reducing turnover than realistic job previews (38, 71).

- Job socialization programs primarily targeted to new employees (who are more likely to leave jobs than are established employees) reduce turnover (82, 88, 124).

- Organizational commitment increases following training (118) and may have reciprocal effects on training success (28, 118).

- Dissention within heterogeneous work groups accelerates departures (90).

- The presence of demographically diverse work groups accelerates turnover (48, 70, 120).

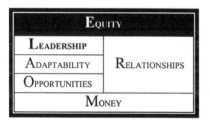

LEADERS are responsible for the continuation of the organization and its work from the past into perpetuity.

Good organizations are marked by capable leadership at the top; great organizations are marked by capable leadership throughout. Leaders bring to their organizations their personal visions and their values, which promote and sustain the standards of conduct and performance and direct the activity of all. Leaders at all levels do their personal best, and they select competent personnel, and provide the encouragement, guidance, skills and resources needed for all to do their best.

- Employees who believe that their jobs are secure have greater affective commitment to the organization (9).

- Greater job security reinforces the inclination of employees to stay (23).

- The sense of interdependence between superiors and their subordinates (**LEADER**-member exchange) promotes affective commitment to the organization (67) and extends job tenure (21, 35).

- Poor **LEADER**-member exchange leads to higher rates of turnover (35).

- **LEADERS** who express consideration for employees promote affective commitment to the organization (24, 69).

- **LEADER** supportiveness promotes affective commitment to the organization (85, 130).

- Perceived **LEADER** facilitation decreases perceived job stress (119).

EQUITY at work entails the perception that all employees are being treated fairly by the leaders and managers of the organization.

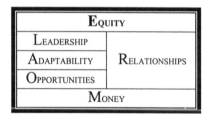

Equity	
Leadership	
Adaptability	Relationships
Opportunities	
Money	

The perception of **EQUITY** is a critical prerequisite of employee job satisfaction and commitment to the organization. The presence in the workforce of persons of with increasingly diverse backgrounds provides a challenge and an opportunity to demonstrate fairness at work.

- The perception of the fairness of organizational policies and employee treatment promotes employee commitment to a greater extent than personal outcome (31, 64, 117).

- The perception that organizational policies in pay (106), drug testing (53), and strategic decision making (52) are fair promotes commitment to the organization.

- Explanations for company policies that are perceived to be fair and adequate (53) promote retention.

EXERCISE 6 provides an opportunity to compare the components of the **MORALE**™ model that your organization does well with those that departing employees cite as problem areas.

SUMMARY

Research findings on why employees leave their jobs and why they stay can reasonably be sorted into the six categories of the **MORALE**™ model for employee job satisfaction, productivity and commitment.

Adequacy of compensation (**MONEY**) is *a* bottom line consideration for employers and employees, alike. But for most employees, compensation is not the most important factor in deciding whether to stay on or leave their jobs.

The perception of fairness at work (**EQUITY**) is a very important determinant of employees' decisions to stay or leave. Its importance is based on the fact that in work settings, the perception of fairness or unfairness is based on an *overall* assessment of **EQUITY** in the areas of **MONEY, OPPORTUNITIES, RELATIONSHIPS, ADAPTABILITY** and **LEADERSHIP**.

EXERCISE 6
MORALE™ COMPONENTS IN PRACTICE

MORALE™ Dimension	Things our organization does in these areas that gain us a good reputation are:	Employees who leave our organization tend to cite shortcomings such as these:
MONEY		
OPPORTUNITIES		
RELATIONSHIPS		
ADAPTABILITY		
LEADERSHIP		
EQUITY		

CHAPTER 5 INVESTING (AND INVESTING IN) NEW EMPLOYEES

Several authors (5, 10, 50, 122) have documented that the early experiences of employees new to an organization have an important impact on the tenure of these employees. The successful management of newcomers' expectations is a critical component of a retention management program because it can help reduce the employee initiated turnover of new employees.

During the SELECTION period the organization should present a realistic picture of the everyday work life of employees who perform the duties for which a candidate is being recruited or considered. Even though the picture that is painted may be far from glamorous, its accuracy will stimulate in the newcomer the perception that the organization is truthful and fair. A false impression risks the opposite perception

During the ORIENTATION and SUPERVISION stages of employee installation, the organization should continue to present realistic assurances of what it can and cannot do for its employees. An important source of information about the organization comes from long-time employees. According to Jones (50), the extent to which newcomers receive positive (investiture) support from seasoned co-workers is associated with commitment to the organization. Positive support includes reinforcement of the new employee's self-esteem. Negative support involves disaffirmation of the employee's positive expectations of the new job experience.

Furthermore, during the ORIENTATION and SUPERVISION stages supervisors and other managers should set low rather than high expectations for employee performance. Although this recommendation may seem contrary to regular practice, it is important for two reasons.

First, during the early stages of employment at a new job employees face the monumental task of trying to understand their organizations (51). For example, they must learn when to ask questions, when to petition for a vacation or a raise in salary, how to uncover the various reward contingencies in an organization and other important prerequisites for career success. All of these activities reduce the amount of time and energy new employees have to perform at their peak levels of productivity.

Second, lower initial performance expectations are more likely to be met, thereby warranting positive feedback between the new employee and his or her supervisor. By systematically raising performance expectations for new employees, supervisors create multiple opportunities to relate with these employees in a positive and constructive manner.

The **SOS** model provides a special retention oriented focus on recommended activities during the SELECTION, ORIENTATION and SUPERVISION phases of new employees' work experiences in the organization.

SELECTION: should assure that the right (and necessary) job is being filled by the best qualified applicant whose limitations are known and taken into account.

To accomplish this, organizations should:

- conduct periodic job analyses;

- select employees who demonstrate a:

    a. high need for achievement;
    b. strong work ethic;
    c. good understanding of their own competence;
    d. predisposition to commitment;
    e. congruence of their own values with those of the organization; and/or
    f. congruence of their own goals with those of the organization;

- offer realistic job previews; and

- communicate realistic expectations regarding the anticipated performance of the employee and the organization.

ORIENTATION: should last long enough to accomplish three organizational requirements:

1. *transmit* to the new employee critical information about the organization, its mission, vision of the future, values, policies and practices;

2. *transport* the new employee from old work relationships to new relationships in this organization; and

3. *transform* the new employee's knowledge, skills, abilities, attributes and preferences into productive work for this organization.

To achieve these results, organizations should regularly perform the following tasks.

- Continue to communicate realistic expectations regarding the anticipated performance of the employee and the organization. The more new employees' early experiences on the job match their prior expectations about the job, the more likely they are to remain on that job (126).

- Invest the new employee in the organization and its goals.

- Minimize or eliminate role ambiguity and role conflict.

- Demonstrate that the organization supports the employee.

SUPERVISION: should shape employees' knowledge, skills, abilities and commitment to:

    a) regularly perform duties consistent with their job assignments; and

    b) contribute to the mission of the organization.

To accomplish this, organizations should:

- continue to communicate realistic expectations regarding the anticipated performance of the employee and the organization;

- continue to minimize or eliminate role ambiguity and role conflict;

- continue to demonstrate that the organization supports the employee;

- express consideration for the employee; and

- provide for early career assessments.

SUMMARY

Newcomers to organizations are especially susceptible to early resignations. The SELECTION-ORIENTATION-SUPERVISION (SOS) model summarizes strategies to successfully incorporate new employees into productive organizational life. This process begins with the selection of the best-qualified candidates for the job and continues with a comprehensive orientation program and supportive supervision.

PART III: THE 4 Rs OF RETENTION MANAGEMENT

In PARTS I and II we have investigated the reasons why some employees leave their jobs, and why some employees stay. In this PART we will focus on the four main components of a comprehensive retention management program focusing on: *R*ates; *R*easons; *R*esponses; and *R*esults.

*R*ates refers to information concerning *who* is leaving, and *how* much it costs to replace them. This information is usually sorted into categories such as: age; gender; racial/ethnic background; level of education; type of work they do; where they work; and how long they worked for the organization. Strategies for collecting and analyzing this information are discussed in CHAPTER 6.

*R*easons refers to the explanations that departing employees give for leaving the organization. Strategies for collecting and analyzing this information, especially exit interviews, are discussed in CHAPTER 7.

Responses refers to the steps organizations take to retain employees who want to leave their jobs. In CHAPTER 8 we will revisit the 12 reasons for leaving one's job most commonly offered on exit interviews[14]. Using these reasons as a framework, we will propose common situations or conditions that lead departing employees to cite these reasons for leaving. Then we will propose some retention interventions that have been demonstrated to be effective in dealing with these conditions and situations.

Results refers to a systematic approach to planning and evaluating the effectiveness of retention intervention programs. Strategies for collecting and analyzing this information are discussed in CHAPTER 9.

---

[14] See pages 4-5.

CHAPTER 6 — RATES: TURNOVER POSITIONS, COSTS AND FREQUENCIES

The first step in managing employee initiated turnover is to identify:

- how many employees are leaving (turnover rates);
- what are their characteristics;
- how long does it take to replace them (duration of vacancies); and
- at what costs (turnover costs)?

TURNOVER RATES

An employee turnover rate is calculated by determining the number of employees who leave their jobs in the organization during a specific time period (# departures), dividing this number by the average number of jobs in the organization (# jobs) for the same time period and multiplying by 100. The result is the rate of employee turnover.

$$\text{Employee turnover rate} = \frac{\text{\# departures}}{\text{\# jobs}} \times 100$$

For example, if 45 persons depart from 300 positions in a one-year period, the annual turnover rate for these jobs is 15%.

Rates of employee turnover are frequently calculated by specific work units and employee characteristics. TABLE 6 presents an example of annual turnover data.

TABLE 6
TURNOVER RATES: AN EXAMPLE

Employee Categories	Turnover Rate
All employees	10.1%
Male	9.8%
Female	10.6%
Caucasian	10.7%
Black	8.5%
18-29 Years Old	17.9%
30-39 Years Old	10.4%
40-49 Years Old	7.5%
50-59 Years Old	4.5%
60+ Years Old	15.9%
<1 year of service	12.9%
1-4 years of service	8.1%
5-10 years of service	6.4%
11-19 years of service	5.1%
20+ years of service	5.7%
Full-Time	10.1%
Part-Time	11.2%
Department A	3.8%
Department B	7.1%
Department C	10.3%
Department D	11.8%
Department E	5.3%
Department F	5.2%
Department G	8.1%
Department H	9.2%
Department I	10.3%
All other Departments	11.2%

In some settings, turnover rates vary depending on factors such as time of year (e.g., at the end of a school year) or the actions of other employers in the area (e.g., hiring freezes). For this reason, turnover data collected and analyzed on a quarterly or monthly basis, as well as annually, will provide better information to managers about the true rates and causes of turnover.

When turnover rates are calculated on a monthly, quarterly and annual basis, current rates can be compared to those from a prior time frame (e.g., March 2000 vs. February 2000 and/or vs. March 1999; 1st quarter 2000 vs. 1st quarter 1999; 2000 vs. 1999, etc.).

DURATION OF VACANCIES

The amount of time that vacated positions are left unfilled (duration of vacancies) is an important indicator of the extent to which employee initiated turnover is a problem for an organization. Quick turnaround in replacing departing employees reduces the impact of turnover on the organization.

The duration of vacancy rate for a particular job category (e.g., nurses, programmers, accountants, French teachers) is the average length of time that positions in that category have been vacant. This rate is calculated by totaling the number of weeks that the positions in the category have been vacant and dividing by the number of vacant positions in the category.

$$\text{Position duration of vacancy rate} = \frac{\text{\# weeks positions in category vacant}}{\text{\# vacant positions in category}}$$

For example, if last month a health care system had eight vacancies for nurses, and these positions had been vacant for a total of 138 weeks, the duration of vacancies rate for nurses would be 17.25 weeks. When duration of vacancies rates are calculated on a monthly, quarterly and annual basis, current rates can be compared to those from a prior time frame (e.g., March 2000 vs. February 2000 and/or vs. March 1999; 1st quarter 2000 vs. 1st quarter 1999; 2000 vs. 1999, etc.).

TURNOVER COSTS

The financial costs of turnover to the organization are often both significant and poorly understood. Four categories of costs need to be considered in determining the overall cost of turnover. They are: *separation costs; inefficiency costs; replacement costs;* and *installation costs.* These costs are detailed in FIGURE 7. Turnover costs are generally calculated by adding the costs for each category and adding the categories together.

A sample worksheet for calculating turnover costs is presented in FIGURE 8.

Turnover rate and turnover cost numbers are important to managers because they help define whether the organization has a problem with turnover, and if so, where that problem is centered.

For example, an organization may have a small overall rate of turnover, but a high rate of turnover among hard to replace employees. Or the high rate may be among employees who are very expensive to replace. In these situations, although overall turnover is relatively low, the organization has a turnover problem.

FIGURE 7
CATEGORIES OF TURNOVER COSTS

Separation costs:	• Administration of termination • Exit interview
Inefficiency costs:	• Overtime • Temporary workers • Lost productivity of departing employee • Reduced productivity of temporary replacement employee(s) • Reduced productivity of co-workers • Lost work opportunities
Replacement costs:	• Advertising • Recruiter • Agency fees • Application processing • Screening • Interview - including candidate travel and interviewer(s) • Selecting • Compensation differential
Installation costs:	• Relocation • Employee processing • Orientation • Training • Productivity differential

The employee turnover cost (for one departing employee or a category of employees) is calculated by adding the above costs, as shown here:

Separation costs
+ Inefficiency costs
+ Replacement costs
+ Installation costs

Employee turnover cost

FIGURE 8
SAMPLE TURNOVER COSTS WORKSHEET

Separation Costs:

Administration of termination	Human resource specialist time **x** rate/hour
Exit interview	[Exit interviewer time **x** rate/hour] + [departing employee time **x** rate/hour]
	Total Separation Costs:

Inefficiency Costs:

Overtime	Number of hours **x** rate/hour
Temporary workers	Number of hours **x** rate/hour
Lost productivity of departing employee	[Productivity before intent to leave – productivity after intent to leave] **x** value of the productivity units
Reduced productivity of temporary replacement employee(s)	[Productivity of departed employee – productivity of temporary replacement employees] **x** value of the productivity units
Reduced productivity of co-workers	[Productivity prior to departure – productivity after departure] **x** value of the productivity units
Lost work opportunities	[Number of opportunities expected – number of opportunities achieved] **x** value of each opportunity
	Total Inefficiency Costs:

Replacement Costs:

Advertising	Advertising costs
Recruiter	Recruiter time **x** rate/hour
Application processing	Processor time **x** rate/hour
Screening	Screening time **x** rate/hour
Interviewer(s)	Interviewer time **x** rate/hour
Candidate travel	Travel reimbursement costs
Selecting	Number of selectors **x** selector time **x** rate/hour
Agency fees	Costs for employment agency
Compensation differential	New employee compensation – departed employee compensation
	Total Replacement Costs:

Installation Costs:

Relocation	Relocation costs
Employee processing	Processing costs (tests, employment paperwork)
Orientation	[New hire orientation time **x** rate/hour] + [Orienter time **x** rate/hour]
Training	[New hire training time **x** rate/hour] + [Trainer time **x** rate/hour]
Productivity differential	Productivity of former employee – productivity of new employee
	Total Installation Costs:
	TOTAL TURNOVER COSTS:

ESTABLISH RETENTION MANAGEMENT BASELINES AND TARGET OUTCOMES

Turnover rates and turnover costs are also important elements in the evaluation of the effectiveness of a retention management program. Current rates and costs serve as baseline indictors of the effectiveness of retention management efforts. Desired rates and costs become target outcomes for future retention interventions.

The establishment of target outcomes (or objectives) performs two important functions for a retention management program. First, it helps focus the entire activity by identifying valuable and achievable benefits that the organization hopes to accomplish through its retention management efforts. It does this by requiring managers to select from a wide array of possible outcomes those results that are both desirable and achievable. Second, it supplies the basis and criteria for evaluating the effectiveness of retention interventions.

Establish baselines

What are your organization's historic and current employee initiated turnover rates and costs? How are these rates and costs determined? Do they vary based on the time of month or year? Are there recurring patterns of turnover that correspond to specific actions or conditions? What are these specific actions and conditions? How do they impact on turnover in your organization?

TABLE 7 presents sample retention management target outcomes and baselines derived from a variety of organizations. EXERCISE #7 provides a blank form on which to record base rates, target rates, current rates and progress data for your retention management program.

TABLE 7

SAMPLE RETENTION MANAGEMENT TARGET OUTCOMES AND BASELINES

Target outcomes	Base rate/basis	Target rate/basis		
Turnover: overall	14% annually	8% annually		
Turnover: pay grade 11	16% annually	6% annually		
Turnover: Ohio region	18% annually	14% annually		
Turnover: <180 days on job	25% annually	15% annually		
Tenure: overall	Mean = 814 weeks	Mean = +30 weeks		
Tenure: <180 days on job	Mean = 20 weeks	Mean = +10 weeks		
Recruitment time: overall	Mean = 34 weeks	Mean = 9 weeks		
Recruitment time: IT	Mean = 48 weeks	Mean = 15 weeks		
Turnover costs: overall	$865,000/year	$400,000/year		
Turnover costs: sales	$128,000/year	$38,000/year		
Turnover costs: production	$426,000/year	$200,000/year		
Overtime costs	$88,500	$40,000		

EXERCISE 7
SAMPLE RETENTION MANAGEMENT TARGET OUTCOMES AND BASELINES FORM

Target outcomes	Base rate/basis	Target rate/basis	

Establish target outcomes

What changes do you want to accomplish in the area of employee initiated turnover? What retention management outcomes would you consider to be successful?

A properly designed retention management program will focus the attention of the organization on specific areas for improvement. These areas and the desired outcomes will be specified in advance and communicated to all persons who are responsible for achieving them or contributing to their success.

These target outcomes should meet the five SMART criteria set forth in FIGURE 9. Some examples of retention management target outcomes are presented in FIGURE 10.

FIGURE 9
SMART CRITERIA FOR TARGET OUTCOMES
AND CHARACTERISTICS

SMART Criteria	Characteristics
Specific	Outcomes precisely state the performance levels that are to be achieved.
Measurable	These outcomes can be quantified and a means is available to measure results.
Assign-able	The organization has available to it a person (or persons) who can be made responsible for achieving the outcome.
Realizable	The organization can achieve the outcome with current or planned resources.
Time limited	A date for achieving the outcome is set in advance and communicated to all persons responsible for its achievement.

FIGURE 10
SAMPLE RETENTION MANAGEMENT TARGET OUTCOMES

Reduce overall turnover
Reduce turnover for specific
- positions
- sites
- categories of employees

Extend tenure for specific
- positions
- sites
- categories of employees

Reduce duration of vacancies
- positions
- sites
- categories of employees

Reduce the costs associated with turnover
- Separation costs
  - administration of termination
  - exit interview
- Inefficiency costs
  - overtime
  - temporary workers
  - lost productivity
  - lost work opportunities
- Replacement costs
  - advertising
  - recruiting
  - screening/selecting
  - applicant processing
  - compensation differential
- Installation costs
  - relocation
  - employee processing
  - orientation/training
  - production differential

SUMMARY

The effectiveness of retention management programs are measured by comparing organizational performance on relevant turnover indicators after the introduction of retention interventions to organizational performance prior to these improvements. Three important indicators in this area are:

1. turnover rates, especially among groups of employees who merit retention attention[15];

2. the duration of vacancies, especially among groups of employees who merit retention attention; and

3. the costs associated with replacing employees who depart.

Retention target outcomes based on these indicators serve as the goals and/or objectives of a retention management effort.

---

[15] See pages 76-77.

CHAPTER 7 *R*EASONS: EXIT INTERVIEWS

WHAT DO WE MEAN WHEN WE SPEAK OF AN *EXIT INTERVIEW*?

The term *exit interview* means different things in different organizations. Generally, it refers to a meeting between a departing employee and either his or her supervisor or some other representative of management at or near the time of the employee's departure from the organization.

At this time, several things may transpire.

1. They may discuss post employment benefits.

2. The employee may return organization property (e.g., badges, keys, equipment, etc.).

3. The employee may complete necessary paperwork.

4. They may reminisce about the employee's experiences with the organization.

5. The organization may collect standard information on the employee's perception of his or her work experience and/or reasons for leaving.

The first four categories of activities constitute an *exit meeting*. The fifth category is an *exit interview*, whether it is conducted during the exit meeting or at another time. Information about a departing employee's perception of his or her work experience and/or reasons for leaving can also be collected through an exit interview survey.

The information generated through exit interviews, whether administered through a person-to-person interview or a survey, are valuable to the organization and its managers, to the departing employees, and to employees who remain.

Exit interviews are valuable to the organization and its managers when they:

- generate information about employees' reasons for leaving;

- provide a "heads up" about ongoing and/or emerging human resource problems;

- document things that work (and do not work) within the organization; and/or

- provide information about competitors and their practices.

Exit interviews are valuable to departing employees when they:

- provide a sense of closure for employees;

- satisfy employees' desire to give feedback on their job experience; and/or

- provide information that may benefit their friends at work and/or other co-workers who stay behind.

Exit interviews can be valuable to those employees who remain if managers learn about problems that adversely affect employees, and reduce or eliminate these problems.

CHARACTERISTICS OF A COMPREHENSIVE EXIT INTERVIEW SYSTEM

Recent research (3) has identified ten characteristics of a comprehensive exit interview system. These characteristics are presented and described in EXERCISE 8.

EXERCISE 8
COMPREHENSIVE EXIT INTERVIEW SYSTEM CHARACTERISTICS

In the column to the right, check the extent to which these characteristics are met in your organization.

1. **Interviewers are trained.** Interviewers trained to conduct the exit interview are better able to identify reasons for departure and seek clues that will aid the organization's effort to lower turnover.
   - ❏ Yes
   - ❏ Somewhat
   - ❏ No

2. **Interviews are universally conducted.** All employees (or all employees in specific categories) should participate in an exit interview. This practice will ensure a more complete understanding of reasons for employee turnover throughout the organization.
   - ❏ Yes
   - ❏ Somewhat
   - ❏ No

3. **Interviews are standardized.** The exit interview should be comprised of a set of core questions asked of all departing employees. A consistent approach will help generate reliable results
   - ❏ Yes
   - ❏ Somewhat
   - ❏ No

4. **Interviews focus on the work experience.** The focus of the exit interview should be on the reason(s) for departing the job, including feedback on the work environment. The exit interview session should not be used to point out employee faults, criticize the reasons for departure, or to ask the employee to reconsider the decision to leave.
   - ❏ Yes
   - ❏ Somewhat
   - ❏ No

5. **Interviewers are independent.** Employees who separate voluntarily often are not comfortable expressing the true reason(s) for their departure to their supervisors and/or other managers. An independent interviewer can help minimize this discomfort.

❑ Yes
❑ Somewhat
❑ No

6. **The exit interview process is integrated with other employee relations efforts.** The exit interview process can be used to track known reasons for employee dissatisfaction and determine relationship(s) between employee dissatisfaction and employee turnover.

❑ Yes
❑ Somewhat
❑ No

7. **Exit interview data is centrally managed.** To understand why turnover occurs, it is important that all exit interview information is available to management. Collecting and maintaining results in a central location makes the information easily available.

❑ Yes
❑ Somewhat
❑ No

8. **Reports are reviewed regularly.** Reports of exit interview findings that include an analysis of data trends should be prepared and distributed regularly. Supervisors and senior managers should routinely review these reports.

❑ Yes
❑ Somewhat
❑ No

9. **Reports are used in decision making.** The information collected from exit interviews can provide valuable insights into the workings of the organization. The best use of exit interview information is to develop practical solutions for turnover related problems.

❑ Yes
❑ Somewhat
❑ No

10 **Results are acted upon.** Acting on solutions developed from exit interview information and measuring the effect of planned changes can limit future unplanned turnover.

❑ Yes
❑ Somewhat
❑ No

CHOICES IN THE DESIGN OF EXIT INTERVIEWS

The *why* of exit interviews

There are many reasons to administer standardized exit interviews with departing employees. They include, but are not limited to, the following:

* to find out why employees are quitting;
* to learn about competitors;
* to identify problem areas in the organization;
* to assist recruitment efforts (including re-hiring former employees);
* to measure the success of retention management initiatives;
* it is a cost effective form of employee attitude study;
* employees expect it; and/or
* senior managers require it.

The *how* of exit interviews

There are two primary ways to formally collect exit interview information: through a person-to-person interview and through a written survey. Both approaches are referred to as *exit interviews* throughout this book.

A person-to-person interview can be conducted in person at work or some other convenient place. It can also be conducted by telephone or other remote technology.

Surveys can be completed on the spot and returned to the person who will record and report departing employees' comments. Or they can be mailed or e-mailed to the person administering the survey, if it is completed elsewhere.

The *who* of exit interviews

Exit interview information can be collected from any number of employees by a variety of staff or by outside professionals. For example, supervisors, HR staff, managers, other employees, or 3rd party exit interviewers can conduct person-to-person exit interviews or administer exit surveys.

Exit interview information can be collected from many different categories of employees. They include all departing employees, a random sample of departing employees, only voluntarily departing employees, employees who are difficult to replace (positions warranting *retention attention*)[16], and those who are transferring within the organization.

Who: Transferring employees

Transferring employees frequently are not given the opportunity to complete an exit interview or survey. Yet, many employees transfer positions within an organization for the same reasons that other employees leave the organization. These reasons may be uncovered in an exit interview with transferring employees.

Who: Some employees deserve *retention attention*

Exit interview studies do not have to collect information from all departing employees. Special attention should be given to determine reasons why the types of employees listed in EXERCISE 9, those employees who deserve retention attention, decide to leave. Supervisors and recruiters are good sources of information for developing a list of employees for retention attention.

---

[16] These positions may correspond to the *high potential* and *talent pool* employees described by Woodruffe (131).

EXERCISE 9
POSITIONS DESERVING RETENTION ATTENTION

In the right column (Examples), list positions in your organization that may correspond to the types of jobs that deserve retention attention in your industry and market.

Employees who...	Examples
are difficult to replace	
are costly to replace	
are effective performers	
will influence others to leave	
may work for a competitor	
have specialized knowledge/ experience	
are essential members of important organization teams	
are difficult/costly to get job ready	
are crucial to current business	
are crucial to future business	

The *when* of exit interviews

Most exit interviews are given shortly before the employee leaves the organization or shortly thereafter. The exit interview can be given at other times as well. For example, it can be administered a few months after the employee leaves.

Two somewhat unconventional times to collect information about the reasons why employees leave are *at hiring* and at *any time* during employment.

When: At hiring

Research has amply documented that many persons leave their jobs to avoid specific work related conditions or achieve specific work related outcomes[17]. Supervisors and other managers who inquire at hiring how and why job candidates decided to leave their former jobs, learn early in their employees' tenure the conditions that cause them to leave or stay on the job. Managers can use this information to create the conditions and offer the opportunities that will make the organization an attractive work place to these new employees.

When: Anytime

Exit interviews can collect departing employees' assessments of many aspects of their work experiences. Some of these aspects are displayed in Column A of Table 8, and in Figures 11 and 12. Coincidentally, many organizations collect similar information from current employees through routine employee surveys, focus groups, suggestion boxes and conversations with employees (cf. Table 8, Column B and the employee survey in Figure 11)[18].

---

[17] See Chapter 2 for a more detailed explanation of this point.

[18] See CHARACTERISTIC #6 in EXERCISE 8 on page 74.

TABLE 8
TYPES OF EMPLOYEE FEEDBACK INFORMATION

A Employee opinions	B How collected on an ongoing basis	C How collected at departure
Adequacy of compensation	Performance Review; Focus Group; Compensation & Benefit Study; Employee Attitude Survey	Exit Interview
Satisfaction with one's supervisor	360° Evaluation; Focus Group; Employee Attitude Survey	Exit Interview
Job-person match	Job Analysis; Performance Review	Exit Interview
Supportiveness of co-workers	Performance Review; Focus Group; Employee Attitude Survey	Exit Interview
General working conditions	Performance Review; Suggestion Box; Focus Group; Employee Attitude Survey	Exit Interview
Overall job satisfaction	Performance Review; Focus Group; Employee Attitude Survey	Exit Interview
Confidence in management	Performance Review; Focus Group; Employee Attitude Survey	Exit Interview
Commitment to quality	Performance Review; Focus Group; Employee Attitude Survey	Exit Interview
Need for training/development	Performance Review; Training Needs Assessment	Exit Interview
Impact of training programs	Performance Review; Focus Group; Employee Attitude Survey	Exit Interview
Career plans	Performance Review	Exit Interview
Personal circumstances	Performance Review	Exit Interview
Fairness of treatment	Performance Review; Focus Group; Employee Attitude Survey	Exit Interview
Competitors for employees	Word-of-mouth; Focus Group	Exit Interview

Figure 11
CoInS™ Employee Survey

Coordinated Input Systems ™
Employee Attitude Survey

Directions: For each aspect of your job listed below, first circle the numbers to the left that best reflect how satisfied you are with each job aspect in your current job. Then, circle the numbers to the right that best reflect how important each job aspect is to you.

How *satisfied* I am with these aspects of my current job:

How *important* these aspects of my job are to me:

Satisfied: Very little	Some	A fair amount	Quite a bit	A lot	Very much	#	Aspects of my job	Important: Very little	Some	A fair amount	Quite a bit	A lot	Very much
1	2	3	4	5	6	1.	My salary	1	2	3	4	5	6
1	2	3	4	5	6	2.	Company policies and procedures	1	2	3	4	5	6
1	2	3	4	5	6	3.	Being recognized when I do a good job	1	2	3	4	5	6
1	2	3	4	5	6	4.	Company is committed to quality product/service	1	2	3	4	5	6
1	2	3	4	5	6	5.	Having a supportive supervisor	1	2	3	4	5	6
1	2	3	4	5	6	6.	My benefits	1	2	3	4	5	6
1	2	3	4	5	6	7.	Understanding what is expected of me	1	2	3	4	5	6
1	2	3	4	5	6	8.	Having supportive co-workers	1	2	3	4	5	6
1	2	3	4	5	6	9.	Getting the training I need to do my job well	1	2	3	4	5	6

1	2	3	4	5	6	10. Having good communication with my supervisor	6	5	4	3	2	1
1	2	3	4	5	6	11. Job security	6	5	4	3	2	1
1	2	3	4	5	6	12. Having meaningful work to do	6	5	4	3	2	1
1	2	3	4	5	6	13. Being able to balance my work and home life	6	5	4	3	2	1
1	2	3	4	5	6	14. Opportunities for personal/professional development	6	5	4	3	2	1
1	2	3	4	5	6	15. Getting regular feedback on my work	6	5	4	3	2	1
1	2	3	4	5	6	16. Being able to get my work done on time	6	5	4	3	2	1
1	2	3	4	5	6	17. Getting a good orientation to the company	6	5	4	3	2	1
1	2	3	4	5	6	18. Having a fair way to resolve conflicts at work	6	5	4	3	2	1
1	2	3	4	5	6	19. Feeling good about my work	6	5	4	3	2	1
1	2	3	4	5	6	20. Opportunities to advance in the company	6	5	4	3	2	1
1	2	3	4	5	6	21. Being able to do the job I was hired to do	6	5	4	3	2	1
1	2	3	4	5	6	22. Ease in getting to and from work	6	5	4	3	2	1
1	2	3	4	5	6	23. Not having to do the work of my co-workers	6	5	4	3	2	1
1	2	3	4	5	6	24. Being treated fairly by my supervisor	6	5	4	3	2	1
1	2	3	4	5	6	25. Getting help to do my job easier or better	6	5	4	3	2	1

Figure 12
CoInS™ Exit Survey

Coordinated Input Systems™ Exit Survey

Directions: For each aspect of your job listed below, first circle the numbers to the left that best reflect how satisfied you were with each job aspect in your current job. Then, circle the numbers to the right that best reflect how important each job aspect is to you.

How satisfied I was with these aspects of my work at ..						Aspects of my job	How important these aspects of my job are to me:					
Very little	Some	A fair amount	Quite a bit	A lot	Very much		Very little	Some	A fair amount	Quite a bit	A lot	Very much
1	2	3	4	5	6	1. My salary	1	2	3	4	5	6
1	2	3	4	5	6	2. Company policies and procedures	1	2	3	4	5	6
1	2	3	4	5	6	3. Being recognized when I do a good job	1	2	3	4	5	6
1	2	3	4	5	6	4. Company is committed to quality product/service	1	2	3	4	5	6
1	2	3	4	5	6	5. Having a supportive supervisor	1	2	3	4	5	6
1	2	3	4	5	6	6. My benefits	1	2	3	4	5	6
1	2	3	4	5	6	7. Understanding what is expected of me	1	2	3	4	5	6
1	2	3	4	5	6	8. Having supportive co-workers	1	2	3	4	5	6
1	2	3	4	5	6	9. Getting the training I need to do my job well	1	2	3	4	5	6

1	2	3	4	5	6		1	2	3	4	5	6
1	2	3	4	5	6	10. Having good communication with my supervisor	1	2	3	4	5	6
1	2	3	4	5	6	11. Job security	1	2	3	4	5	6
1	2	3	4	5	6	12. Having meaningful work to do	1	2	3	4	5	6
1	2	3	4	5	6	13. Being able to balance my work and home life	1	2	3	4	5	6
1	2	3	4	5	6	14. Opportunities for personal/professional development	1	2	3	4	5	6
1	2	3	4	5	6	15. Getting regular feedback on my work	1	2	3	4	5	6
1	2	3	4	5	6	16. Being able to get my work done on time	1	2	3	4	5	6
1	2	3	4	5	6	17. Getting a good orientation to the company	1	2	3	4	5	6
1	2	3	4	5	6	18. Having a fair way to resolve conflicts at work	1	2	3	4	5	6
1	2	3	4	5	6	19. Feeling good about my work	1	2	3	4	5	6
1	2	3	4	5	6	20. Opportunities to advance in the company	1	2	3	4	5	6
1	2	3	4	5	6	21. Being able to do the job I was hired to do	1	2	3	4	5	6
1	2	3	4	5	6	22. Ease in getting to and from work	1	2	3	4	5	6
1	2	3	4	5	6	23. Not having to do the work of my co-workers	1	2	3	4	5	6
1	2	3	4	5	6	24. Being treated fairly by my supervisor	1	2	3	4	5	6
1	2	3	4	5	6	25. Getting help to do my job easier or better	1	2	3	4	5	6

The information that organizations collect from their current employees may also be relevant to the reasons why some of them later decide to leave, or why other employees are leaving now. Unfortunately these data are often not compared with the results of the organizations' exit interview studies.

One remedy for this lost opportunity is to ask the *same* questions about employees' work experiences in *both* employee attitude surveys *and* exit interviews. An example of a coordinated approach to identifying the attitudes of employees about critical aspects of their jobs, both while employed and at departure is shown in the matching employee attitude survey and exit survey presented in Tables 11 and 12.

The *what* of exit interviews

Exit interviews should collect the departing employee's primary and any secondary reasons for leaving. Information about the employment experience, such as opinions about supervision, management, communication and working conditions are frequently collected as well. The types of information presented in Column A of TABLE 8 can also be collected in an exit interview.

The exit interview or survey also provides an opportunity to learn what the employee liked best and least about working for the organization, and what he or she will be doing next.

Some clients request that 3rd party exit interviews probe employees on the salary/benefits package they will be receiving at their new jobs. The ability to engage in probes like this is an advantage of a person-to-person interview approach.

EXERCISE 10 provides a summary checklist of choices in the design of an exit interview and survey.

EXERCISE 10
EXIT INTERVIEW CHECKLIST

Check all that apply in your organization.

How we collect exit interview information

Person-to-person method	Survey method
❑ Face-to-face interview	❑ Hand in
❑ Telephone interview	❑ Mail back
❑ Remote technology	❑ Internet/Intranet
❑ Other	❑ Other

Who collects information	Who gives the information
❑ Supervisors	❑ All employees
❑ HR staff	❑ A sample of employees
❑ Managers	❑ Specific employees
❑ Other employees	❑ Voluntarily or involuntarily
❑ 3rd party exit interviewers	departing employees
❑ Other	❑ Transferring employees
	❑ Other

When we administer an exit interview

❑ A few months after the employee leaves
❑ Shortly after the employee leaves
❑ After giving notice of leaving and before the employee departs
❑ Any time during employment
❑ At hiring
❑ Other

What we collect during an exit interview

❑ Primary and any secondary reasons for departure
❑ Opinions about supervisors, managers, communication, working conditions, etc.
❑ What the employee liked best and least about his or her job
❑ What new job the employee is taking (if any)
❑ Other

PREDICTING TURNOVER

The primary reason for conducting exit interviews is to retain valued workers. Exit interviews help retain valued workers primarily by identifying areas of their work experiences that departed employees felt led them to leave their organizations. Such information can identify for managers areas for improvement that can avert further employee initiated turnover among the remaining employees.

Developing turnover predictors

1. Using an exit interview approach, identify the primary reasons for turnover among different groups in the organization.

2. Incorporate in employee attitude and/or opinion surveys, or other questionnaires that are routinely administered to employees, questions about the situations or conditions that departing employees state lead to employee initiated turnover.

3. Track employee survey responses for changes (positive or negative) in employee satisfaction on questions about the situations or conditions that have been identified as leading to turnover among selected employee groups.

4. Report findings (positive or negative) to key managers for possible retention intervention efforts.

SUMMARY

Person-to-person exit interviews and exit surveys with departing employees using standardized questions on the employee's work experiences with the organization and their reasons for leaving are the most effective way to gain an understanding of the causes of employee initiated turnover in an organization.

These forms of exit interviews are very robust and allow the organization to uncover much information about the experience of being an employee. In many organizations, similar information is available through routine employee attitude studies (such as surveys or focus groups) but often the findings generated through employee surveys and exit interviews are not coordinated to reduce employee initiated turnover.

By focusing on employees who are difficult to hire or important to retain, organizations can tailor their exit interview strategy and later intervention efforts to retaining these key employees.

CHAPTER 8 RESPONSES: RETENTION INTERVENTIONS

The way an organization responds to employee initiated turnover depends on many factors, including the organization's history and culture, the general economic conditions in the region(s) where it operates and the organization's:

- current situation and expected future conditions;
- ability to learn the reasons why employees leave;
- capacity to respond to employee expectations and requirements;
- reputation among potential job applicants.

In EXERCISE 11 we re-present[19] the 12 reasons for leaving most often offered on exit interviews (Column A). In Column B, we list some common situations or conditions that lead departing employees to cite these reasons. In Column C, we list retention interventions that have been effective in dealing with the conditions and situations that lead to employee initiated turnover. In Column D list intervention(s) you may include in a retention management plan.

---

[19] See pages 4-5.

EXERCISE 11
ANALYSIS OF POSSIBLE RETENTION INTERVENTIONS

A: Reason	B: Possible Cause(s)	C: Potential Remedies	D: Planned Corrections
1. Advancement opportunities	A. Turned down for promotion B. No opportunities in my area of expertise C. No opportunities where I would like to live D. Advancement only by leaving this organization	a. Job rotation b. Job enrichment c. Career development d. Career paths e. Commuting accommodations	
6. Geographic location of the job	A. Region of the country/ world B. Size of the community C. Commuting distance/time D. Community characteristics/ amenities E. Spouse relocation F. Unsafe area to work	a. Match job assignments to employee preferences b. Match geographic assignments to employee preferences c. Commuting options d. Better physical security for employees	

	Causes	Solutions
7. Immediate supervisor	A. Unrealistic expectations B. Not qualified to supervise C. Unfair treatment D. Treats others preferentially E. Little interest in employees' duties/work F. Unfair/inaccurate performance appraisal G. Poor listener H. Poor communicator	a. 360° evaluation of managers and supervisors b. Supervisory training c. Communication skills training d. Job coaching for supervisors e. Disciplinary action, if warranted
14. Job itself	A. Not the job I accepted B. No sense of accomplishment C. Job responsibilities D. Work load/pace E. Work content/schedule F. Changing job competencies G. Changed employee competencies H. Conflicts with personal values/goals	a. Job analysis b. Review/revise recruitment materials c. Realistic job preview d. Competency-based training e. Job enrichment f. Career planning

A: Reason	B: Possible Cause(s)	C: Potential Remedies	D: Planned Corrections
17. Job stress	A. Workload B. Work/personal life balance C. Involuntary work changes D. Inflexible rules/schedules E. Stressful co-workers/ managers F. Organization culture	a. Flexible work schedules b. Job sharing c. Stressor reduction d. Stress management training e. Reassignment	
25. Organization rules/policies/ procedures	A. Organization policies and procedures too restrictive B. Organization policies and procedures carried out unevenly/unfairly C. Organization policies and procedures do not support/ protect employees D. Lack of empowerment	a. Review/revise organization policies/procedures b. Manager/supervisor training c. Organizational climate study	

26. Performance appraisal or performance appraisal methods	A. Not administered B. Evaluations unfairly/ unevenly administered C. Rater is not competent to rate employee D. Not recognized for contributions E. Others take/are given credit for my contributions F. Insufficient performance feedback G. Contributions stolen	a. Redesign performance appraisal system (e.g., employee initiated) b. Rater training c. Employee recognition activities/events
28. Personal relationship with co-workers	A. Antagonistic atmosphere B. Non-collegial atmosphere C. Lack of workgroup supportiveness D. Have to do others' work	a. Means to fairly resolve conflicts b. Promote teamwork c. Encourage "best friend at work" arrangements

A: Reason	B: Possible Cause(s)	C: Potential Remedies	D: Planned Corrections
33. Salary/ general com-pensation	A. Inadequate for my expectations/conditions B. Inadequate for industry/region C. Inflexible D. Low compared with competitors E. No opportunity for adjustment/advancement	a. Compensation and benefit study b. Salary adjustments c. Benefit adjustments d. Bonuses/special incentives	
34. Training I received	A. Lack of development opportunities B. Inadequate training C. Limited exposure to other training opportunities	a. Training needs assessment b. Employee orientation c. On-the-job training d. Other training e. Job rotation	

35. Upper level management	A. Lack of vision/direction B. Conflict with core values C. Leadership style D. Little contact with employees E. Little interest in duties/ work of employees F. Leader perceived as non-supportive	a. Long range planning b. Share planning outcomes with employees c. Align organization's and employees' values d. Select employees whose values are consistent with the organization e. Supportive leadership f. Expanded leader-employee interaction	
40. Working conditions	A. Physical environment B. Too little staff for work C. Organization culture D. Inadequate resources to get the job done E. Obsolete equipment	a. Provide a safe, clean, well lighted, well illuminated work place b. Treat employees fairly c. Provide good equipment and supplies d. Provide adequate staffing	

SUMMARY

The findings of research on employee initiated turnover and commitment provide a rich array of strategies for reducing turnover among groups of employees with high rates of turnover, long delays in filling vacancies and/or high costs associated with replacing them.

In this CHAPTER, the 12 reasons for leaving most commonly offered on exit interview surveys serve as an outline for elaborating on employees' reasons for leaving, as well as recommending strategies to retain key employee groups.

RESULTS: MEASURING THE EFFECTIVENESS OF RETENTION MANAGEMENT EFFORTS

TABLE 9 re-presents the sample data first presented in CHAPTER 6. Here current turnover data is entered with a calculation of the effectiveness of recent efforts to reduce employee initiated turnover, including calculations of the amount of progress made toward achieving the stated target outcomes. Information on progress realized toward achieving the stated retention management outcomes should be used to direct the choice of revised retention management outcomes and strategies.

For example, the reasons for the great progress (+150%) shown for the Ohio region should be analyzed and understood. Seemingly successful approaches there could be exported to other regions, unless the true basis for the reduction in turnover is a situation outside the organization's control such as a rise in the unemployment rate in that area.

TABLE 9
SAMPLE RETENTION MANAGEMENT OUTCOMES AND BASELINES, CURRENT DATA AND PROGRESS REPORT

Target outcomes	Base rate/basis	Target rate/basis	Current rate/basis	Progress
Turnover: overall	14% annually	8% annually	10% annually	67% of goal
Turnover: pay grade 11	16% annually	6% annually	14 % annually	20% of goal
Turnover: Ohio region	18% annually	14% annually	12% annually	150% of goal
Turnover: <180 days on job	25% annually	15% annually	28% annually	-30% of goal
Tenure: overall	Mean = 814 weeks	Mean = +30 weeks	Mean = 844 weeks	100% of goal
Tenure: <180 days on job	Mean = 20 weeks	Mean = +10 weeks	Mean = +8 weeks	80% of goal
Recruitment time: overall	Mean = 34 weeks	Mean = 9 weeks	Mean = 12 weeks	88% of goal
Recruitment time: IT	Mean = 48 weeks	Mean = 15 weeks	Mean = 36 weeks	36% of goal
Turnover costs: overall	$865,000/year	$400,000/year	$825,000/year	9% of goal
Turnover costs: sales	$128,000/year	$38,000/year	$98,000/year	33% of goal
Turnover costs: production	$426,000/year	$200,000/year	$328,000/year	43% of goal
Overtime costs	$88,500	$40,000	$52,600	74% of goal

Some data elements interact to tell a more complete story than they would alone. In this example, the percentage of overall turnover drops by only 67% of the goal, while the average tenure of departing employees achieves 100% of its goal. This data may suggest that the employees who are leaving tend to have been on the job longer than those who made up the baseline group. Or it could suggest that the target outcomes for these two data categories may need to be better coordinated.

The rate of turnover among recently hired employees (<180 days on the job) is reported to have gone up. Such activity may add costs to new hire orientation and training activities.

Finally, overall turnover cost has declined by only 8% of its target objective, while overtime cost has declined to 74% of its target objective. These data suggest that efforts to reduce overtime have been relatively successful, but they have had a marginal impact on overall turnover costs. New strategies may be needed to better contain turnover costs. Such an effort may require the development of other cost-related target outcomes such as new employee orientation and training.

If further analysis proves that costs of orientating and training new employees significantly contribute to the poor showing on overall cost reduction, the solution may be found in intensified efforts to retain new employees. Strategies to accomplish this may include better job analyses, candidate screening, realistic job previews or newcomer investiture activities.

As this limited sample of cost and turnover statistics makes clear, the more data elements that are systematically tracked against target outcomes, the easier it will be to select the best retention interventions.

Exercise 12 presents a sample grid for the recording of target outcome, rate and progress data for your organization.

EXERCISE 12
SAMPLE RETENTION MANAGEMENT TARGET OUTCOMES AND BASELINES, CURRENT DATA
AND PROGRESS REPORT FORM

Target Outcomes	Base rate/basis	Target rate/basis	Current rate/basis	Progress

SUMMARY

Retention target outcomes based on indicators such as turnover rates, the duration of vacancies caused by employee initiated turnover, and the costs of turnover are matched against current performance on these indicators after the introduction of retention interventions.

Partial successes in achieving these target outcomes may serve as the basis for continued use of these retention intervention strategies. Minimal or no gains should serve as a basis for re-thinking the causes of employee initiated turnover, and their solutions.

Continued or new retention management approaches begin a new cycle of intervention, measurement and analysis which should continue until levels of employee initiated turnover are acceptable to the organization.

To Bring Back

Throughout this book we have relied on the significant findings of research on employee commitment and turnover for our recommendations on managing employee retention. In this final section, we combine these findings with managerial best practices to describe a comprehensive approach to retention management.

STEP 1: FIND OUT WHAT WORK *MEANS* TO YOUR EMPLOYEES.

Your employees are working for your organization to accomplish purposes that are important to *them*. These purposes may be simple or complex, humble or grand. By relating[20] with your employees, by asking them why they work at this job at this time in their lives, you can bring back to the organization that information to develop better ways to retain them.

---

[20] The verb *to relate*, and its derivatives, *relating* and *relationship* have as their root the Latin word that means *to bring back*.

- **Determine why your key employees are working for your organization.** Identify which of your employees work for your organization because they want to (affective commitment), feel they ought to (normative commitment) or need to (continuance commitment).

- **Discover what situations may cause them to consider leaving.** Identify what your key employees consider as shocks to their current work situations, as well as their scripts and value, strategic and tactical images. It is estimated that as many as 75% of employees who have experienced a shock at work either call upon a pre-existing script or evaluate the shock in terms of their personal value, strategic and tactical images[21] (60).

- **Design opportunities that promote employees' value, strategic and tactical images.** Supervisors who are aware of their employees' shocks, scripts, and images are best able to retain these employees in the event of a shock by helping their employees to develop scripts that do not lead directly to departure or by better aligning the employee's images and those of the organization.

STEP 2: CREATE A RETENTION ORIENTED ENVIRONMENT.

Most employees share a common view of conditions that promote retention. These conditions can be partially achieved through the application of these processes and procedures.

- **Establish and maintain the perception (and practice) of fair treatment.** Dealing with employees in such a way that they feel they are being treated fairly is one of the most important ways to keep valued employees.

---

[21] That is, they pursue either Paths 1, 2 or 3 in the unfolding model of Lee and associates. See pages 22-26 for more information on this point.

- **Model retention-oriented behavior.** Leaders and other managers should model behavior that promotes commitment including: (a) demonstrating their own commitment to the organization; (b) acting with fairness toward all employees; and (c) earning the respect of all with whom they deal.

- **Screen and select applicants based on the results of periodic job analyses.** Valid and reliable job analyses provide the persons who are responsible for screening and selecting new employees with objective criteria on the knowledge, skills, abilities and other personal characteristics necessary for a newcomer to make a successful adjustment to his or her new job.

- **Give qualified candidates a realistic job preview.** Realistic job previews reduce unwanted turnover in two ways. First, they discourage applicants to pursue employment if the working conditions and expectations are undesirable to them. Second, persons who consciously select jobs are more likely to remain on the job, even if their jobs entail some undesirable aspects.

- **Properly incorporate new employees into the organization.** Because much unwanted turnover occurs in the early stages of an employee's career with an organization, pay proper attention to new employees' needs to optimize acceptance and minimize uncertainty.

- **Communicate low rather than high expectations for performance** through the recruitment, selection and early socialization stages of employment so that newcomers' expectations will not be disconfirmed (126). Early negative experiences with the organization will impede the development of affective commitment.[22]

---

[22] See especially CHAPTER 5, pages 49-52 for more information on this point.

- **Give positive feedback early and often.** To perform effectively in the organization, new employees must:

  1. learn the criteria by which success is gauged;
  2. develop the ability to see themselves as others see them; and
  3. understand how others evaluate their behavior (8).

  Early and frequent positive feedback provides additional information that employees (new and established) can use to make corrections in their behavior and increase their chances of achieving their personal goals, and the performance goals set by the organization.

- **Minimize involuntary job or task changes.** Involuntary job changes tend to strain the bond between the employee and the job of their selection, making transfers to other jobs, including jobs outside the organization, easier to consider and accept.

- **Offer opportunities for advancement and enrichment.** The perception that an organization promotes from within is an important tactic for enhancing affective commitment among current employees. Many organizations have adopted flatter, less hierarchical organizational designs, thereby reducing opportunities for advancement. Where the opportunities for advancement are few, employees should be provided with opportunities to *enhance* their knowledge, skills, abilities and experiences.

- **Arrange frequent interaction between employees and their leaders, managers and supervisors.** Frequent contact between employees and managers, especially the employee's direct supervisors and senior managers, promotes affective commitment to the organization and provides the managers with important information on the current levels of job satisfaction/dissatisfaction among key employees.

- **Enhance affective and normative commitment without expanding continuance commitment.** Employees who maintain a continuance level of commitment toward the organization tend to not be as productive as employees who have affective or normative commitment.

STEP 3: IDENTIFY EMPLOYEES FOR *RETENTION ATTENTION*.

Full-fledged person-to-person exit interview studies can become expensive if conducted with all departing employees. If the cost of such studies is an impediment to them being conducted, focusing this approach on select employees may prove to be a very cost-effective way to manage retention in the organization. Such employees include those who:

- are difficult to replace; and/or
- are costly to replace; and/or
- are effective performers; and/or
- will influence others to leave; and/or
- may go to work for a competitor; and/or
- have specialized knowledge/experience; and/or
- are essential members of important organizational teams; and/or
- are difficult/costly to get job ready; and/or
- are crucial to current business; and/or
- are crucial to future business.

STEP 4: FIND OUT WHEN AND WHY KEY EMPLOYEES DECIDE TO LEAVE.

Employees' reasons for leaving should be continuously monitored on several accounts. For example, the reasons why employees leave vary among departing employees and across time periods. Also, retention interventions may significantly reduce or eliminate some categories for leaving thereby raising the frequency of other reasons.

* **Continuously measure employees' attitudes about their work experiences.** Regular employee attitude studies, especially ones intentionally linked to exit interviews, can help supervisors and other managers forecast turnover activity in their areas of responsibility and take corrective actions to limit turnover.

* **Conduct regular exit interviews.** Regular exit interviews, especially person-to-person interviews that permit interviewer probing of reasons for departure, provide the best source of information on ways to reduce turnover in an organization.

* **Conduct follow-up studies of former employees.** Some employees' perceptions of their former work experiences change after several months. For some employees the expectations that led them to accept an offer of employment from another organization (or from school or retirement) are not realized.

Follow-up exit interview studies will provide another view of employees' experiences with the organization, and may offer an opening to re-recruit valuable former employees.

STEP 5: RE-RECRUIT YOUR *CURRENT* KEY EMPLOYEES.

The best place to begin a retention management program is with your current employees. Reducing turnover immediately reduces turnover-related costs freeing up some of these funds to make working conditions more attractive for all employees.

With this strategy in mind, consider re-recruiting strategies for your current employees, and record them below:

If recruiters offer your employees...	*then offer them...*
• better pay/benefits/perks	•
• better working conditions	•
• more recognition	•
• the job of their choosing	•
• job stability	•
• job variety	•
• role clarity	•
• little/less stress	•
• opportunity for advancement	•
• skill development	•
• fair treatment	•
• flexible/responsive company policies	•
• new or better workplace relationships	•
• other: _____	•

STEP 6: CULTIVATE COMMITMENT TO THE ORGANIZATION'S MISSION.

Managers at all levels should actively promote employee commitment to the organization and its mission. Strategies for accomplishing this include the following steps.

1. Assess levels of members' awareness of the mission, commitment to the mission and ability to perform in support of the mission.

2. Provide appropriate motivation and training to promote the awareness, commitment and ability needed to carry out the mission.

3. Share the mission or some aspect of the mission with all members.

4. Create an environment that supports the mission and members' efforts to contribute to the mission.

5. Link the mission to the roles members play in accomplishing the mission. Wherever possible, encourage participation in implementing the mission.

6. Make sure that the benefits and/or outcomes of carrying out the mission are known. These include the benefits to the benefactors of the organization and the benefits to the employee.

STEP 7: ROUTINELY EVALUATE THE RESULTS OF RETENTION MANAGEMENT EFFORTS.

Finally, every good management plan should have an evaluation strategy to measure progress toward organizational goals and objectives. To accomplish this:

- collect turnover data;
- calculate the costs of turnover;
- establish target outcomes;
- establish cost and turnover data baselines;
- develop and introduce interventions;
- measure and analyze results;
- develop and implement alternatives; and
- invest retention management savings in further retention management efforts.

SUMMARY

In our PREFACE, we stated that this is a book about treating employees right. Throughout the preceding CHAPTERS, we have referred to significant findings of research on employee commitment and turnover. These findings have generated ideas about how to treat employees right, so that their employing organizations can retain productive workers, and deal fairly with other employees.

Despite "How To" books that claim to have *the answer* to reducing employee turnover, our research suggests that there are *many* best ways to keep valued employees. These ways have in common the desire to treat employees right, and the recognition that supervisors and other managers can come to learn how to treat employees right by relating with their employees.

In this final section, we summarize our own ideas on a comprehensive approach to retention management, based both on research findings and other managerial best practices. They are presented as ideas and suggestions *to bring back* to your regular work responsibilities. They include ideas and suggestions about how to relate to employees who you would like to stay, so that you can learn about them and the things they need and want from their work situations.

The key to overturning turnover involves both understanding what work means to your employees, and helping them achieve that meaning in your organization. Overturning turnover requires that supervisors and other managers relate to their employees in ways that recognize and value employees as individuals. In a world where employee contributions are often treated as a commodity, good people will choose to make their contributions where they – both the people and the contributions – are seen as unique and worthy of respect.

What are the best ways to keep the employees who you want to stay? Now that you know why some employees leave and why some employees stay, ask the employees who you want to stay, "What are the best ways to keep employees like you?" They will tell you. Moreover, if you ask them while they are still working with you, many of your employees will be more inclined to stay *because* you asked.

REFERENCES

1. Abelson, M.A. (1987). Examination of avoidable and unavoidable turnover. *Journal of Applied Psychology,* *72*, 382-86.

2. Ahr, P.R. (2000). Relationships and the reasons for turnover in organizations. *Missouri Municipal Review, 65* (3), 15-17.

3. Ahr, T.B. (1998). The survey says.... *CPContext, 2* (2), 1-4.

4. Allen, N.J. & Meyer, J.P. (1990a). The measurement and antecedents of affective, continuance, and normative commitment to the organization. *Journal of Occupational Psychology, 63*, 1-18.

5. Allen, N.J. & Meyer, J.P. (1990b). Organizational socialization tactics: A longitudinal analysis of links of newcomers' commitment and role orientation. *Academy of Management Journal, 33*, 847-858.

114

6. Allen, N.J. & Meyer, J.P. (1996). Affective, continuance and normative commitment to the organization: An examination of construct validity. *Journal of Vocational Behavior, 49*, 252-276.

7. Angle, H.L. & Lawson, M.B. (1994). Organizational commitment and employees' performance ratings: Both type of commitment and type of performance count. *Psychological Reports, 75*, 1539-1551.

8. Ashford, S.J. (1986). Feedback-seeking in individual adaptation: A resource perspective. *Academy of Management Journal, 29* (3), 465-487.

9. Ashford, S.J., Lee, C., & Bobko, P. (1989). Content, causes and consequences of job insecurity: A theory-based measure and substantive test. *Academy of Management Journal, 32*, 803-829.

10. Ashforth, B.E. & Saks, A.M. (1996). Socialization tactics: Longitudinal effects on newcomer adjustment. *Academy of Management Journal, 39*, 149-178.

11. Axelrod, R. (1984). *The evolution of cooperation.* New York: Basic Books.

12. Baker, H.E. & Feldman, D.C. (1990). Strategies of organizational socialization and their impact on newcomer adjustment. *Journal of Managerial Issues, 11*, 198-212.

13. Bashaw, E.R. & Grant, S.E. (1994). Exploring the distinctive nature of work commitments: Their relationships with personal characteristics, job performance, and propensity to leave. *Journal of Personal Selling and Sales Management, 14*, 41-56.

14. Bateman, T.S. & Strasser, S. (1984). A longitudinal analysis of the antecedents of organizational commitment. *Academy of Management Journal, 27,* 95-112.

15. Baugh, S.G. & Roberts, R.M. (1994). Professional and organizational commitment among engineers: Conflicting or complementing? *IEEE Transactions on Engineering Management, 41,* 108-114.

16. Beach, L.R. (1997). *The psychology of decision making.* Thousand Oaks, CA: Sage.

17. Brief, A.P. & Aldag, R.J. (1989). The economic functions of work. In G. Ferris and K. Rowland (Eds.) *Research in Personnel and Human Resources Management, 7.* Greenwich, CT: JAI Press.

18. Buchanan, B. (1974). Building organizational commitment: The socialization of managers in work organizations. *Administrative Science Quarterly, 19,* 533-546.

19. Bycio, P., Hackett, R.D., & Allen, J.S. (1995). Further assessments of Bass's (1985) conceptualization of transactional and transformational leadership. *Journal of Applied Psychology, 80,* 468-478.

20. Cotton, J.L., & Tuttle, J.M. (1986). Employee turnover: A meta-analysis and review with implications for research. *Academy of Management Review, 11,* 55-70.

21. Dansereau, F. Jr., Graen, G., & Haga, W.J. (1975). A vertical dyad linkage approach to leadership within formal organizations. *Organizational Behavior and Human Performance, 13,* 46-48.

22. Darden, W.R., Hampton, R., & Howell, R.D. (1989). Career versus organizational commitment: Antecedents and consequences of retail salespeoples' commitment. *Journal of Retailing, 65,* 80-106.

23. Davy, J.A., Kinicki, A.J., & Scheck, C.L. (1991). Developing and testing a model of survivor responses to layoffs. *Journal of Vocational Behavior, 38,* 302-317.

24. DeCottis, T.A. & Summers, T.P. (1987). A path analysis of a model of the antecedents and consequences of organizational commitment. *Human Relations, 40,* 445-470.

25. Donovan, L. (1980). What nurses want. *RN,* 43, 22-30.

26. Dunham, R.B., Grube, J.A., & Castaneda, M.B. (1994). Organizational commitment: The utility of an integrative definition. *Journal of Applied Psychology, 79,* 370-380.

27. Eisenberger, R., Fasolo, P., & Davis-LaMastro, V. (1990). Perceived organizational support and employee diligence, commitment and innovation. *Journal of Applied Psychology, 75,* 51-59.

28. Facteau, J.D., Dobbins, G.H., Russell, J.E.A., Ladd, R.T., & Kudish, J.D. (1995). The influence of general perceptions of the training environment on pretraining motivation and perceived training transfer. *Journal of Management, 21,* 1-25.

29. Feldman, D.C. (1988). *Managing careers in organizations.* Glenview, IL: Scott, Foresman.

117

30. Fisher, C.D. (1986). Organizational socialization: An integrative review. In G. Ferris and K. Rowland (Eds.) *Research in Personnel and Human Resources Management, 4.* Greenwich, CT: JAI Press.

31. Folger, R. & Konovsky, M.A. (1989). Effects of procedural and distributive justice on reactions to pay raise decisions. *Academy of Management Journal, 32,* 115-130.

32. Gaertner, K.N. & Nollen, S.D. (1989). Career experiences, perceptions of employment practices, and psychological commitment to the organization. *Human Relations, 42,* 975-991.

33. Gellatly, I.R. (1995). Individual and group determinants of employee absenteeism: Test of a causal model. *Journal of Organizational Behavior, 16,* 469-485.

34. Giacalone, R.A. & Duhon, D. (1991). Assessing intended employee behavior in exit interviews. *Journal of Psychology, 125* (1), 83-90.

35. Graen, G.B. & Scandura, T.A. (1986). A theory of dyadic career reality. In G. Ferris and K. Rowland (Eds.) *Research in Personnel and Human Resources Management, 4.* Greenwich, CT: JAI Press.

36. Gregersen, H.B. (1993). Multiple commitments at work and extra-role behavior during three stages of organizational tenure. *Journal of Business Research, 26,* 31-47.

37. Gregersen H.B. & Black, J.S. (1992). Antecedents to commitment to a parent company and a foreign operation. *Academy of Management Journal, 35,* 65-90.

38. Griffeth, R.W. (1985). Moderation of the effects of job enrichment by participation: A longitudinal field experiment. *Organizational Behavior and Human Decision Processes, 35,* 73-93.

39. Guzzo, R.A., Noonan, K.A., and Elron, E. (1994). Expatriate managers and the psychological contract. *Human Resources Management, 33,* 447-462.

40. Hackett, R.D., Bycio, P., & Hausdorff, P.A. (1994). Further assessments of Meyer and Allen's (1991) three-component model of organizational commitment. *Journal of Applied Psychology, 79,* 15-23.

41. Hinrichs, J.R. (1975). Measurement of reasons for resignation of professionals: Questionnaire versus company and consultant exit interviews. *Journal of Applied Psychology, 60,* 530-532.

42. Hom, P.W. & Griffeth, R.W. (1995). *Employee turnover.* Cincinnati, OH: South-Western College Publishing.

43. Huey, F.L. & Hartley, S. (1988). What keeps nurses in nursing. *American Journal of Nursing, 88,* 181-188.

44. Hulin, C.L. (1991). Adaptation, persistence and commitment to organizations. In *Handbook of industrial and organizational psychology,* M.D. Dunnette and L.M. Hough, (Eds.) 2d ed. Vol 2. Palo Alto, CA: Consulting Psychologists Press.

45. Hulin, C.L., Roznowski, M, & Hachiya, D. (1985). Alternative opportunities and withdrawal decisions: Empirical and theoretical discrepancies and an integration. *Psychological Bulletin, 97,* 233-250.

46. Ingram, T.N., Lee, K.S. & Skinner, S. (1989). An empirical assessment of salesperson motivation, commitment and job outcomes. *Journal of Personal Selling and Sales Management, 9*, 25-33.

47. Ippolito, R.A (1991). Encouraging long-term tenure: Wage tilt or pension? *Industrial and Labor Relations Review, 4*, 520-535.

48. Jackson, S.E., Brett, J.F., Sessa, V.I., Cooper, D.M., Julin, J.A., & Peyronnin, K. (1991). Some differences make a difference: Individual dissimilarity and group heterogeneity as correlates of recruitment, promotions, and turnover. *Journal of Applied Psychology, 76*, 675-689.

49. Johnston, G.P. & Snizek, W. (1991). Combining head and heart in complex organizations: A test of Etzioni's dual compliance structure hypothesis. *Human Relations, 44*, 1255-1272.

50. Jones, G.R. (1986). Socialization tactics, self-efficacy, and newcomers' adjustments to organizations. *Academy of Management Journal, 29* (2), 262-279.

51. Katz, R. (1980). Time and Work: Toward an Integrative Perspective. In L.L. Cummings & B.M. Staw (Eds.), *Research in Organizational Behavior, 2*. Greenwich, CN: JAI Press.

52. Kim, W.C. & Mauborgne, R.A. (1993). Procedural justice, attitudes, and subsidiary top management compliance with multinationals' corporate strategic decisions. *Academy of Management Journal, 36*, 502-528.

53. Konovsky, M.A. & Cropanzano, R. (1991). Perceived fairness of employee drug testing as a predictor of employee attitudes and job performance. *Journal of Applied Psychology, 76,* 698-707.

54. Lawler, E.E. (1971). *Pay and organizational effectiveness: A psychological view.* New York: McGraw-Hill.

55. Lawler, E.E. (1992). Affective attachment to nested groups: A choice process theory. *American Sociological Review, 57,* 327-339.

56. Lee, T.W. (1999). *Using qualitative methods in organizational research.* Thousand Oaks, CA: Sage.

57. Lee, T.W., Ashford, S.J., Walsh, J.P., & Mowday, R.T. (1992). Commitment propensity, organizational commitment, and voluntary turnover: A longitudinal study of organizational entry processes. *Journal of Management, 18,* 15-32.

58. Lee, T.W. & Maurer, S.D. (1997). The retention of knowledge workers with the unfolding model of voluntary turnover: *Human Resource Management Review, 7,* 247-275.

59. Lee, T.W. & Mitchell, T.R. (1994). An alternative approach: The unfolding model of voluntary employee turnover. *Academy of Management Review, 19*: 51-89.

60. Lee, T.W., Mitchell, T.R., Holtom, B.C., McDaniel, L.S., & Hill, J.W. (1999). The unfolding model of voluntary turnover: A replication and extension. *Academy of Management Journal, 42,* 450-462.

61. Lee, T.W., Mitchell, T.R., Wise, L., & Fireman, S. (1996). An unfolding model of voluntary employee turnover. *Academy of Management Journal, 39,* 5-36.

62. Lefkowitz, J. & Katz, M.L. (1969). Validity of exit interviews. *Personnel Psychology, 22* (4), 44-46.

63. Leong, S. M., Randall, D.M. & Cote, J.A. (1994). Exploring the organizational commitment-performance linkage in marketing: A study of life insurance salespeople. *Journal of Business Research, 29,* 7-63.

64. Lind, E.A. & Tyler, T.R. (1986). *The social psychology of procedural justice.* New York: Plenum.

65. Major, D.A., Kozolowski, S.W.J., Chao, G.T., & Gardner, P.D. (1995). A longitudinal investigation of newcomer expectations, early socialization outcomes, and the moderating effects of role development factors. *Journal of Applied Psychology, 80,* 418-431.

66. March, J.G., & Simon, H.A. (1958). *Organizations.* New York: Wiley.

67. Marsh, R.M. & Mannari, H. (1977). Organizational commitment and turnover: A predictive study. *Administrative Science Quarterly, 22,* 57-75.

68. Maslow, A.H. (1954). *Motivation and personality.* New York: Harper & Row.

69. Mathieu, J.E. & Zajak, D. (1990). A review and meta-analysis of the antecedents, correlates, and consequences of organizational commitment. *Psychological Bulletin, 108,* 171-194.

70. McCain, B.E., O'Reilly, C., & Pfeffer, J. (1983). The effects of departmental demography on turnover: The case of a university. *Academy of Management Journal, 26,* 626-641.

71. McEvoy, G.M. & Cascio, W.F. (1985). Strategies for reducing employee turnover: A meta-analysis. *Journal of Applied Psychology, 70,* 342-353.

72. McEvoy, G.M. & Cascio, W.F. (1987). Do good or poor performers leave? A meta-analysis of the relationship between performance and turnover. *Academy of Management Journal, 30,* 744-762.

73. Meyer, J.P. & Allen, N.J. (1991). A three-component conceptualization of organizational commitment. *Human Resource Management Review, 1,* 61-89.

74. Meyer, J.P. & Allen, N.J. (1997). *Commitment in the workplace: Theory, research and application.* Thousand Oaks, CA Sage.

75. Meyer, J.P., Allen, N.J., & Smith, C.A. (1993). Commitment to organizations and occupations: Extension and test of the three-component conceptualization. *Journal of Applied Psychology, 78,* 538-551.

76. Meyer, J.P., Bobocel, D.R., & Allen, N.J. (1991). Development of organizational commitment during the first year of employment: A longitudinal study of pre- and post-entry influences. *Journal of Management, 17,* 717-733.

77. Meyer, J.P., Paunonen, S.V., Gellatly, I.H., Goffin, R.D., & Jackson, D.N. (1989). Organizational commitment

and job performance: It's the nature of the commitment that counts. *Journal of Applied Psychology, 74,* 152-156.

78. Miceli, M.P. & Lane, M.C. (1991). Antecedents of pay satisfaction: A review and extension. In G. Ferris and K. Rowland (Eds.) *Research in Personnel and Human Resources Management, 9.* Greenwich, CT: JAI Press.

79. Miceli, M.P., Jung, I., Near, J.P., & Greenberger, D.B. (1991). Predictors and outcomes of reactions to pay-for-performance plans. *Journal of Applied Psychology, 76,* 508-521.

80. Mignerey, J.T., Rubin, R.B., & Gorden, W.I., (1995). Organizational entry: An investigation of newcomer communication behavior and uncertainty. *Communication Research, 22,* 54-85.

81. Mitchell, O.S. (1983). Fringe benefits and the cost of changing jobs. *Industrial and Labor Relations Review, 37,* 70-78.

82. Mobley, W. H. (1982). *Employee turnover: Causes, consequences, and control.* Reading, MA: Addison-Wesley.

83. Moorman, R.H., Niehoff, B.P., & Organ, D.W. (1993). Treating employees fairly and organizational citizenship behavior: Sorting the effects of job satisfaction, organizational commitment, and procedural justice. *Employee Responsibilities and Rights Journal, 6,* 209-225.

84. Morris, J.H. & Steers, R.M. (1980). Structural influences on organizational commitment. *Journal of Vocational Behavior, 17,* 50-57.

85. Mottaz, C.J. (1988). Determinants of organizational commitment. *Human Relations, 41*, 467-482.

86. Mowday, R.T., Porter, L.W., & Dubin, R. (1974). Unit performance, situational factors, and employee attitudes. *Organizational Behavior and Human Performance, 12,* 231-248.

87. Mowday, R.T., Porter, L.W., & Steers, (1982). *Organizational linkages: The psychology of commitment, absenteeism and turnover.* San Diego, CA: Academic Press.

88. Murname, R.J., Singer, J.D., & Willet, J.B. (1988). The career paths of teachers. *Educational Researcher, 17,* 22-30.

89. Nouri, H. (1994). Using organizational commitment and job involvement to predict budgetary slack: A research note. *Accounting Organization and Society, 19,* 289-295.

90. O'Reilly, C.A., Caldwell, D.F., & Barnett, W.P. (1989). Work group demography, social integration and turnover. *Administrative Science Quarterly, 3,* 21-37.

91. Organ, D.W. & Ryan, K. (1995). A meta-analytic review of attitudinal and dispositional predictors of organizational citizenship behavior. *Personnel Psychology, 48,* 775-802.

92. Pearce, J. L. (1993). Toward an organizational behavior of contract laborers: Their psychological involvement and effect on employee coworkers. *Academy of Management Journal, 36,* 1082-1096.

93. Premack, S.L., & Wanous, J. (1985). A meta-analysis of realistic job preview experiments. *Journal of Applied Psychology, 70,* 706-719.

94. Price, J.L. (1977). *The study of turnover.* Ames, IA: Iowa State University Press.

95. Price, J.L. (1989). The impact of turnover on the organization. *Work and Occupations, 16,* 461-473.

96. Price, J.L. & Mueller, C.W. (1981). A causal model of turnover for nurses. *Academy of Management Journal, 24,* 543-565.

97. Price, J.L. & Mueller, C.W. (1986*). Absenteeism and turnover of hospital employees.* Greenwich, CT: JAI Press.

98. Randall, D.M., Fedor, D.B., & Longenecker, C.O. (1990). The behavioral expression of organizational commitment. *Journal of Vocational Behavior, 36,* 210-224.

99. Reichers, A.E. (1986). A review and reconceptualization of organizational commitment. *Academy of Management Review, 10,* 465-476.

100. Reilly, R.R., Brown, B., Blood, M., & Malatesta, C.Z. (1981). The effects of realistic previews: A study and discussion of the literature. *Personnel Psychology, 3,* 823-834.

101. Rhodes, S.R., & Steers, R.M. (1981). Conventional vs. worker-owned organizations. *Human Relations, 12,* 1013-1035.

102. Rosse, J.G. & Hulin, C.L. (1985). Adaptation to work: An analysis of employee health, withdrawal and change. *Organizational Behavior and Human Decision Processes, 36,* 324-347.

103. Rusbult, C.E. & Farrell, D. (1983). A longitudinal test of the investment model: The impact of job satisfaction, job commitment, and turnover of variations in rewards, costs, alternatives, and investments. *Journal of Applied Psychology, 68*, 429-438.

104. Sager, J.K. & Johnston, M.W. (1989). Antecedents and outcomes of organizational commitment: A study of salespeople. *Journal of Personal Selling and Sales Management, 9*, 30-41.

105. Saks, A.M. (1995). Longitudinal field investigation of the moderating and mediating effects of self-efficacy on the relationship between training and newcomer adjustment. *Journal of Applied Psychology, 80*, 211-225.

106. Schaubroeck, J., May, D.R., & Brown, F.W. (1994). Procedural justice explanations and employee reactions to economic hardship: A field experiment. *Journal of Applied Psychology, 79*, 455-460.

107. Scholl, R.W., Cooper, E.A., & McKenna, J.F. (1987). Referent selection in determining equity perceptions: Differential effects on behavioral and attitudinal outcomes. *Personnel Psychology, 40*, 113-124.

108. Shore, L.M., & Tetrick, L.E. (1991). A construct validity study of the Survey of Perceived Organizational Support. *Journal of Applied Psychology, 76*, 637-643.

109. Shore, L.M. & Wayne, S.J. (1993). Commitment and employee behavior: Comparison of affective and continuance commitment with perceived organizational support. *Journal of Applied Psychology, 78*, 774-780.

110. Sigardson, K.M. (1982). Why nurses leave nursing: A survey of former nurses. *Nursing Administrative Quarterly, 7* (Fall), 20-24.

111. Smith, P.C., Kendall, L.M., & Hulin, C.L. (1969). *The measurement of satisfaction in work and retirement.* Chicago: Rand McNally.

112. Somers, M.J. (1995). Organizational commitment, turnover, and absenteeism: An examination of direct and interaction effects. *Journal of Organizational Behavior, 16,* 49-58.

113. Staw, B.M. (1980). The consequences of turnover. *Journal of Occupational Behavior, 1,* 253-273.

114. Steers, R.M. & Mowday, R.T. (1981). Employee turnover and predecision accommodation processes. In L. Cummings & B. Staw (Eds.), *Research in Organizational Behavior, 3.* Greenwich, CT: JAI Press.

115. Stumpf, S.A. & Dawley, P.K. (1981). Predicting voluntary and involuntary turnover using absenteeism and performance indices. *Academy of Management Journal, 2,* 148-163.

116. Sweeney, P.D., McFarlin, D.B., & Inderrieden, E.J. (1990). Using relative deprivation theory to explain satisfaction with income and pay level: A multistudy examination. *Academy of Management Journal, 33,* 423-426.

117. Sweeney, P.D. & McFarlin, D.B. (1993). Workers' evaluations of the "ends" and the "means": An examination of four models of distributive and procedural justice. *Organizational Behavior and Human Decision Processes, 55,* 23-40.

118. Tannenbaum, S.I., Mathieu, J.E., Salas, E., & Cannon-Bowers, J.A. (1991). Meeting trainees' expectations: The influence of training fulfillment on the development of commitment, self-efficacy, and motivation. *Journal of Applied Psychology, 76,* 759-769.

119. Tetrick, L.E. (1992). Mediating effect of perceived role stress: A confirmatory analysis. In J.C. Quick, L.R. Murphy, & J.J. Hurrell, (Eds.), *Stress and Well-Being at Work.* Washington, D.C.: American Psychological Association.

120. Tsui, A.S., Egan, T.D., & O'Reilly C.A. (1992). Beyond simple demographic effects: The importance of relational demography in superior-subordinate dyads. *Academy of Management Journal, 32* (2), 402-423.

121. Vancouver, J.B., Millsap, R.E., & Peters, P.A. (1994). Multilevel analysis of organizational goal congruence. *Journal of Applied Psychology, 79,* 666-679.

122. Van Maanen, J. & Schein, E.H. (1979). Toward a theory of organizational socialization. In B. Shaw (Ed.), *Research in Organizational Behavior, 1,* (pp.209-264). Greenwich, CT: JAI Press.

123. Vancouver, J.B., & Schmitt, N.W. (1991). An exploratory examination of person-organization fit: Organizational goal congruence. *Personnel Psychology, 44,* 333-352.

124. Wanous, J.P. (1980*). Organizational entry: Recruitment, selection and socialization of newcomers.* Reading, MA: Addison-Wesley.

125. Wanous, J.P. (1992). *Organizational entry*, 2d ed. New York: Addison-Wesley.

126. Wanous, J.P., Poland, T.D., Premack, S.L., & Davis, K.S. (1992). The effects of met expectations on newcomer attitudes and behaviors: A review and meta-analysis. *Journal of Applied Psychology, 77*, 288-297.

127. Weick, K.E. (1995). *Sensemaking in organizations*. Thousand Oaks, CA: Sage.

128. Whitehead, M. (1998). 'Recruit in haste, repent at leisure,' survey warns. *People Management, 9*, 13.

129. Williams, C.R. & Livingstone, L.P. (1994). Another look at the relationship between performance and voluntary turnover. *Applied Psychological Measurement, 9*, 1-26.

130. Withey, M. (1988). Antecedents of value based and economic organizational commitment. *Proceedings of the Annual Meeting of the Administrative Sciences Association of Canada-Organizational Behavior Division, 9*, 124-133.

131. Woodruffe, C. (1999). *Winning the talent war*. West Sussex: Wiley.

Subject Index

ABOUT THE AUTHORS

PAUL R. AHR, PH.D., M.P.A.

is President of The Altenahr Group Ltd.. A licensed clinical psychologist, he has more than 30 years of experience as a clinician, manager and consultant in a variety of private and public sector settings.

Since 1986, Dr. Ahr has developed a nationwide practice of assessment, consultation and training with the leaders and senior managers of corporations, governmental agencies, health care, social services and educational institutions, and not-for-profit organizations.

Dr. Ahr has developed a wide range of survey instruments and diagnostic procedures for identifying the productivity and

THOMAS B. AHR, M.A., PHR

directs Altenahr's exit interview practice. For the past eight years, he has been investigating the meaning of work for employees in a wide variety of public and private organizations. He has extensive experience in designing and implementing a range of employee feedback studies, especially exit interview studies, employee attitude surveys and focus groups.

Thomas Ahr is currently investigating the relationship between the conditions that lead a person to want to leave a job and the reasons they give for leaving on departure.

A champion of the "drilling down" method of person-to-well-being of organizations and the people that they employ and serve.

His insights and approaches in the areas of successful change management, stressor reduction, employee feedback and forecasting behavior at work have been shared with corporations and agencies across the country.

Dr. Ahr has consulted with and trained clients from a wide range of private sector industries, including banks, mortgage and investment companies, insurance companies, high tech companies, corporations involved in manufacturing, mining, wood products, food products and beverages, and real estate companies.

For nearly seven years, Dr. Ahr was Director of the Missouri Department of Mental Health. As Director, he was responsible for the fourth largest workforce in the State, with more than 12,500 employees, who staffed 28 facilities on an around-the-clock schedule.

person interviewing, Mr. Ahr has also identified patterns of non-confrontational exit interview responses that mask employees' real reasons for leaving; reasons that may be of great importance to management.

Based on this experience, Mr. Ahr regularly consults with organizations and conducts training on ways to improve exit interview and other employee feedback processes.

Thomas Ahr has consulted with a wide range of clients in the private sector including banks, mortgage and investment companies; insurance and high tech companies; corporations involved in manufacturing; acute and long term health care organizations; and professional services corporations.

Thomas Ahr was awarded the Master of Arts degree in Management, and is completing the requirements for a Doctorate in that field.

Dr. Ahr has taught at Boston University, and in the Graduate schools of the University of Southern California, the University of Missouri – Columbia), and Virginia Commonwealth University. He currently teaches *Managing Human Resources* in the Executive Master of Health Administration program of the UMC Department of Health Management and Informatics.

ABOUT ALTENAHR

The Altenahr Group, Ltd. (Altenahr) provides assessment, consultation and training services to individuals and organizations on improving the productivity and well-being of organizations and the persons they employ and serve. Founded in 1986, Altenahr operates through its offices in St. Louis, Missouri and Miami Beach, Florida. It is organized into three operating units: Altenahr Consulting, the Center for Productivity and Creativity^{SM}, and the Corporate Psychology Center®.

Altenahr has pioneered the use of large scale *exit interviews* as a mechanism to control turnover and improve overall employee job satisfaction and productivity. Altenahr also conducts an annual study of the exit interview practices of large corporations.

Altenahr's operating units have assisted over 100 organizations by:

- designing employee feedback systems;
- developing and administering exit interviews;
- conducting exit interviews and reviewing and analyzing exit interview data;
- analyzing the causes of turnover;
- training staff on the design, administration and interpretation of exit interviews;

- developing and administering employee attitude and opinion surveys;
- designing and facilitating focus groups;
- converting employee feedback into meaningful recommendations for managers;
- training managers on forecasting behavior in organizations;
- developing performance appraisal systems;
- developing 360° evaluation systems;
- designing succession plans;
- improving the performance of key employees through executive coaching;
- conducting psychological assessments of individual managers;
- assessing groups of individuals for suitability to perform as members of a well-functioning team;
- training key managers on change management strategies;
- training employees to use creativity in problem solving;
- training managers and staff on workplace diversity;
- designing and administering consumer satisfaction surveys; and
- conducting strategic planning and strategic planning retreats.

For more information, please contact:

ALTENAHR

The Altenahr Group, Ltd.

225 S. Meramec – Suite 1032
St. Louis, MO 63105

Telephone: 314-862-3200 Toll free: 877-862-3200
Fax: 314-863-2987 Toll free: 877-862-3202
e-mail: altenahr@cpcontext.com

Quick Reservation/Order Form

Fax orders: Fax this form toll free to: 877-862-3202
Telephone orders: 888-272-0767 (toll free)
E-mail orders: altenahr@cpcontext.com
Postal orders: The Altenahr Group, Ltd.
                      225 S. Meramec – Suite 1032
                      St. Louis, MO 63105

Please send me _____ copies of: ***Overturn Turnover*** by
                      Paul R. Ahr and Thomas B. Ahr.
The price per copy is $14.95 plus $3.00 shipping and handling and
sales tax charges. Contact us for volume discounts.

Method of   Check   Bill me
Payment:
(check one)   Purchase order #_____

**Please send me immediately FREE information on these
services of The Altenahr Group, Ltd.[*]:**

❑ Employee exit interviews
❑ Employee attitude surveys
❑ Retention-Oriented Assessment and Development ™
❑ Other organizational assessment
❑ Consultation
❑ Speaking
❑ Seminars/Training

Name: _____

Organization:: _____

Address: _____

City: _____ State/Zip: _____

Telephone: _____ e-mail: _____

---

[*] Altenahr Group services are provided through the Center for Productivity and
Creativity[SM], Altenahr Consulting and the Corporate Psychology Center ®.

Quick Reservation/Order Form

Fax orders: Fax this form toll free to: 877-862-3202
Telephone orders: 888-272-0767 (toll free)
E-mail orders: altenahr@cpcontext.com
Postal orders: The Altenahr Group, Ltd.
                           225 S. Meramec – Suite 1032
                           St. Louis, MO 63105

Please send me _____ copies of: ***Overturn Turnover*** by Paul R. Ahr and Thomas B. Ahr.
The price per copy is $14.95 plus $3.00 shipping and handling and sales tax charges. Contact us for volume discounts.

Method of Payment: (check one)   Check   Bill me

Purchase order #_____

Please send me immediately FREE information on these services of The Altenahr Group, Ltd.[*]:

☐ Employee exit interviews
☐ Employee attitude surveys
☐ Retention-Oriented Assessment and Development ™
☐ Other organizational assessment
☐ Consultation
☐ Speaking
☐ Seminars/Training

Name: _____

Organization:: _____

Address: _____

City: _____ State/Zip: _____

Telephone: _____ e-mail: _____

---

[*] Altenahr Group services are provided through the Center for Productivity and Creativity[SM], Altenahr Consulting and the Corporate Psychology Center ®.